CW00548694

FREEDOM OF THE DALES

Calver Hill, Reeth and Fremington Edge from Grinton Moor
overleaf: A crisp winter's day above Gordale Scar

Also by Paul Hannon

RAMBLES IN WHARFEDALE
WALKS IN WHARFEDALE
WALKS IN NIDDERDALE
WALKS IN THE CRAVEN DALES
WALKS IN WENSLEYDALE
WALKS IN THREE PEAKS COUNTRY
WALKS IN SWALEDALE
WALKS ON THE HOWGILL FELLS

WALKS IN BRONTE COUNTRY
WALKS IN CALDERDALE

WALKS ON THE NORTH YORK MOORS (WEST)
WALKS ON THE NORTH YORK MOORS (SOUTH)
WALKS ON THE NORTH YORK MOORS (NORTH)

THE WESTMORLAND WAY
THE FURNESS WAY
THE CUMBERLAND WAY

CLEVELAND WAY COMPANION
DALES WAY COMPANION

OVER LAKELAND MOUNTAINS
OVER LAKELAND FELLS

80 DALES WALKS - An omnibus edition (Cordee, Leicester)

EXPLORING THE YORKSHIRE DALES ON FOOT

FREEDOM OF THE DALES

PAUL HANNON

Booze from Fell End Lead Mine, Arkengarthdale

British Library
Cataloguing in Publication Data
Hannon, Paul

Freedom of the Dales: exploring the Yorkshire Dales on foot

1. Walking recreations
2. North Yorkshire (England)

I. Title

796.51094284

ISBN 1-870141-15-6

First published in Great Britain
in 1992 by Hillside Publications
Keighley, West Yorkshire BD22 6NU

Typeset by Carnmor Print & Design, Preston.

Printed in Hong Kong
by the Golden Cup Printing Company

CONTENTS

Introduction 6

1 - WHARFEDALE
Walks 1-8 12

2 - MALHAMDALE
Walks 9-13 40

3 - THREE PEAKS COUNTRY
Walks 14-18 60

4 - THE HOWGILL FELLS
Walks 19-23 78

5 - SWALEDALE
Walks 24-29 100

6 - WENSLEYDALE
Walks 30-35 120

7 - NIDDERDALE
Walks 36-40 140

Notes in conclusion 157

Index 158

INTRODUCTION

FREEDOM OF THE DALES takes an evocative look at 40 outstanding excursions on foot in every corner of the Yorkshire Dales. Rather than holding your hand over every stile, it seeks to be a source of inspiration and reference. Concise essays pick out the more salient features of every walk, allied to the colour photographs which have been carefully selected to portray the Yorkshire Dales in their four-season finery. In conjunction with the outline maps, enough of the routes is suggested to enable them to be plotted on an Ordnance Survey map. This leaves the wanderer free to choose his own means of undertaking the walk, either with OS map, pocket guide, or a combination of the two.

The haphazard boundary of the National Park has not been slavishly followed in these pages, for a work such as this would be failing in its objectives if the likes of upper Nidderdale and the northern Howgill Fells were to be omitted solely on the grounds of bureaucratic dictations. The well-defined individual areas of the Dales fall neatly into seven distinct chapters, each exhibiting very much its own characteristics. Commencing at the southern margin with Wharfedale, the series of walks take a clockwise journey to eventually conclude with its neighbour Nidderdale. Sandwiched in between are the delights of limestone country, long strides on the grassy Howgill Fells and the moors of Swaledale, and the remarkable waterplay of Wensleydale's gills. It is to be hoped that this cross-section of Dales delights will cater for most tastes, and there are no apologies for including many of the better-known features. Malham Cove, Aysgarth Falls and Bolton Abbey are, however, slotted in between a mouth-watering range of less extrovert Dales attractions.

Early mist over Wensleydale

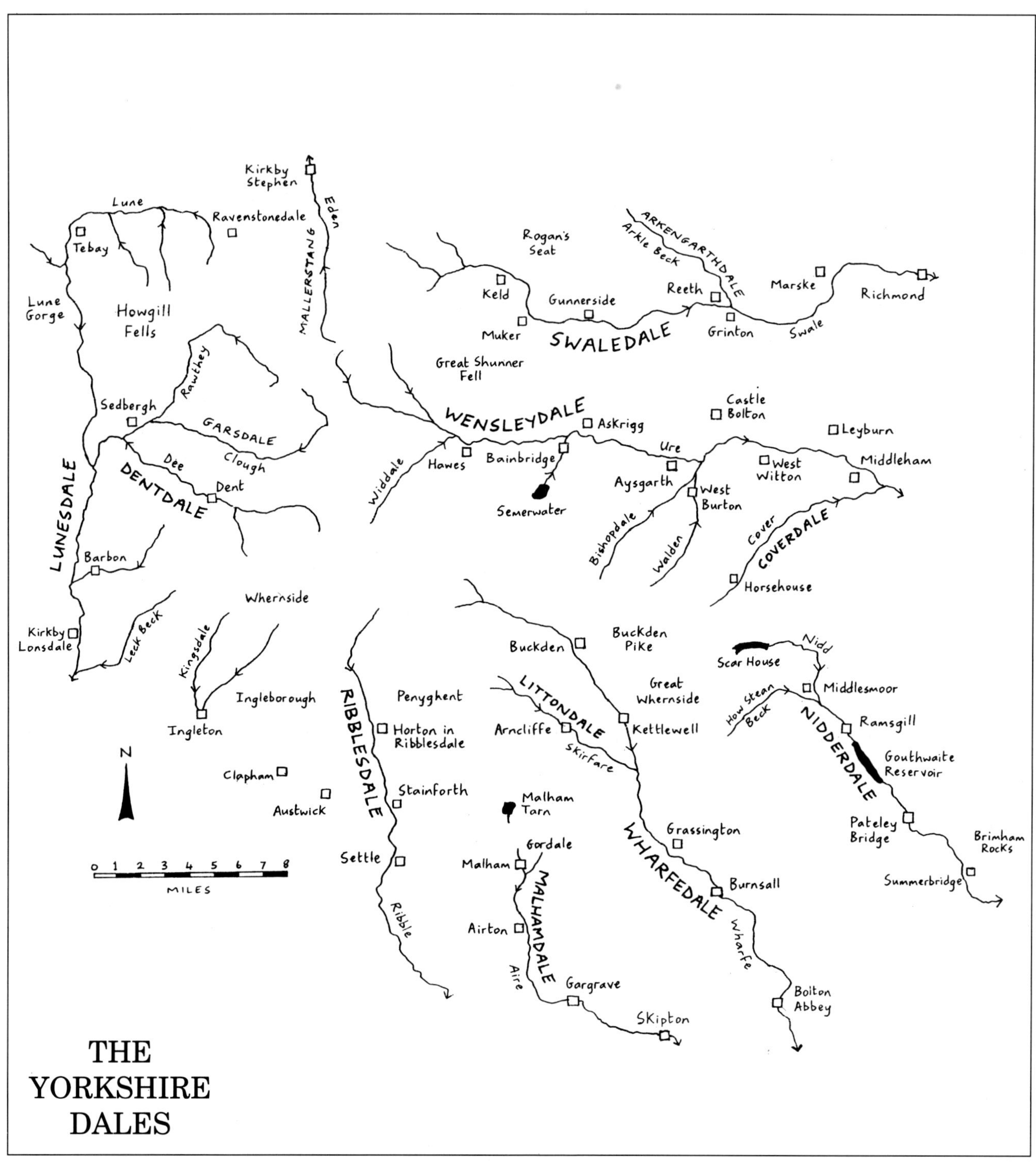

THE YORKSHIRE DALES

THE YORKSHIRE DALES

The Yorkshire Dales are in every sense the true heart of the Pennine Chain. This is the friendly face of England's rippling backbone, flanked by the deep-cut valleys and spacious moorlands of the South Pennines and the massed ranks of the unfrequented mountain-moors of the North Pennines. While certainly not decrying either of these bleak but majestic landscapes, the Dales have a more universal appeal that calls one back again and again.

The Dales boast their own substantial share of rolling uplands, many of which are visited during these walks, though as ascents of the higher mountains could fill a book of their own, these have been left for another day. It is the country below the loftiest contours that draws the majority of walkers to the Yorkshire Dales, and this book deals with all aspects from scented riverbanks, rich meadows and silent woods to cascading gills, dazzling limestone scars, and windswept heather tops. The jewels in the crown, the pride and joy of the Dales, are its villages, tight-knit greystone clusters wrapped around a green or a church. It just wouldn't be the Yorkshire Dales without Dent, Muker or Arncliffe.

One cannot walk long in the Dales without encountering evidence of man's endeavours. In centuries past he laboriously worked lead, coal, stone and a shovelful of lesser known minerals; built dams, railways, and not least of all the arresting lines of drystone walls marching up the fellside or forming crazy patterns on the dale floor. This latter note moves us on to the industry that has survived longest in the Dales, namely farming. The work of the hill farmer is a 365 days a year job, yet in many ways he is chief custodian of this fragile landscape. When enjoying these immemorial scenes we can help maintain them for future generations by treating our playground and his workplace with due respect.

Within these pages you are taken along drove roads and sledgates, pack roads and rail tracks, mine roads and shooters' tracks, Roman roads, monastic roads, and, for good measure, a corpse road. There are even paths formed solely by visitors enjoying the scenery! In conclusion however, the very magic of the Dales lies in the fact that after savouring every one of these walks, you might only then be getting really acquainted with the place. Forty judiciously spread rambles can only skim the surface, even if they do extract a layer of the cream. Countless unsung gems are to be found far from the beaten track, and while I have treated you to some of them, many more await discovery - by me also.

THE GREAT OUTDOORS

As some readers may be encouraged into their first meaningful country walk, it perhaps behoves me to include a little advice on equipment.

Without doubt the most important item is what's on your feet: not necessarily boots at all times, but certainly practical, comfortable footwear. In most situations boots are advisable, to give support, grip, and help keep the feet dry. Having said that, there are many strolls by riverbank and through fields that, in summer at least, will be better enjoyed in something more lightweight, and the ground itself will groan less when not trampled by clod-hopping mountain boots. Next is a good waterproof, for you can only avoid the leaden Pennine skies for so long. Don't be misled by sun-drenched photographs, for I've also fallen for my fair share of grey days. Other items of clothing are really a matter of personal taste, the main point is to ensure sufficient spare clothing is carried, certainly in the colder months, and at all times on the higher fells.

Inside the rucksack make room for food and drink, with a little extra in case you have under-estimated your time. On winter afternoons a torch does not go amiss, as an hour longer than anticipated can easily see you finishing in the gathering gloom. Last but not least, an Ordnance Survey map makes an invaluable companion, particularly if you can read it with confidence. While 1:50,000 Landranger maps are adequate for higher, open country, many walks in the Dales benefit from the finer detail of the 1:25,000 (2½-inch) series. The advantage of the Dales being a popular walking area is that the OS have produced three Outdoor Leisure Maps (representing better value than the normal 1:25,000 series), which happen to cover 80% of the walks in this book. Many walkers will not leave home without a compass either, and while few of these walks are likely to leave you so disorientated as to need one, there are nevertheless occasions where, should the clouds descend, its use might save much unnecessary wasting of time and effort.

With the majority of these walks being within the Yorkshire Dales National Park, its Authority deserves a mention for its excellent record on maintaining and improving the condition of stiles and waymarking on the extensive footpath network.

opposite:
The cobbled streets of Dent

Field path near Hawes

THE WALKS

The 40 walks described are covered in thorough detail (along with many walks not found in these pages) in the following Hillside guides. Occasionally shorter walks have been merged to form a more substantial outing for the purpose of this book.

Walks in Wharfedale 1, 2, 4, 5, 6, 7

Rambles in Wharfedale 3, 8

Walks in the Craven Dales 9, 10, 11, 12, 13

Walks in Three Peaks Country 14, 15, 16, 17, 18
(previously published as Walks in the Western Dales, which omitted 18 but included 19)

Walks on the Howgill Fells 19, 20, 21, 22, 23

Walks in Swaledale 24, 25, 26, 27, 28, 29

Walks in Wensleydale 30, 31, 32, 33, 34, 35

Walks in Nidderdale 36, 37, 38, 39, 40

ACCESS AREAS

Walks 2, 4 and 9 make use of long-standing access agreements over the open spaces of Barden Moor and Barden Fell above Bolton Abbey, and it must be borne in mind that access can be restricted at times of high fire risk or on various days during the grouse shooting season. Closed dates can be obtained in advance from the estate office (Bolton Abbey 227) or the National Park office at Grassington. It might also be useful to know that dogs are not permitted in these areas.

Above Swaledale

INFORMATION

Yorkshire Dales National Park Information Service,
Colvend, Hebden Road, Grassington, Skipton,
North Yorkshire BD23 5LB Tel. (0756) 752748

National Park Centres

Aysgarth Falls (Car Park)
Tel. (0969) 663424

Grassington (Car Park)
Tel. (0756) 752774

Malham (Car Park)
Tel. (0729) 830363

Clapham (Car Park)
Tel. (05242) 51419

Hawes (Station Yard)
Tel. (0969) 667450

Sedbergh (Main Street)
Tel. (05396) 20125

Tourist Information Centres

Horton (Penyghent Cafe)
Tel. (0729) 860333

Kirkby Lonsdale (Main Street)
Tel. (05242) 71437

Leyburn (Thornborough Hall)
Tel. (0969) 23069

Reeth (Swaledale Folk Museum)
Tel. (0748) 84517

Settle (Town Hall)
Tel. (0729) 825192

Ingleton (Community Centre)
Tel. (05242) 41049

Kirkby Stephen (Market St)
Tel. (07683) 71199

Pateley Bridge (Car Park)
Tel. (0423) 711147

Richmond (Friary Gardens)
Tel. (0748) 850252

Skipton (Victoria Square)
Tel. (0756) 792809

Weatherline

Tel. 0898 500 748

CHAPTER ONE **WHARFEDALE**

WALK 1 THE WHARFE AT BOLTON ABBEY 14

WALK 2 THE ASCENT OF SIMON'S SEAT 17

WALK 3 GRIMWITH & TROLLERS GILL 19

WALK 4 THORPE FELL & CRACOE FELL 22

WALK 5 ABOVE THE WHARFE TO STARBOTTON 26

WALK 6 BETWEEN SKIRFARE & WHARFE 30

WALK 7 AROUND PENYGHENT GILL 33

WALK 8 ACROSS HORSE HEAD RIDGE 37

The valley of the Wharfe is perhaps most frequented of any of the Yorkshire Dales, for its proximity to the urban West Riding, an abundance of riverside paths excelled only by Swaledale, and a string of welcoming villages combine to draw large numbers on fine winter weekends as well as the usual summer days. The valley might be divided into two distinct halves in the vicinity of Grassington, a hugely characterful village that is very much the hub of the dale. Downstream the Wharfe flows by many a wooded bank and between high-walled grouse moors where the rough texture of gritstone predominates.

Updale of Grassington limestone country comes into its own, with the inimitable overhang of Kilnsey Crag at the vanguard. On the heights, peaty ground remains true as in other parts of the Dales, while the valley floor's uniformity is underscored by the addition of the river Skirfare from the important side-valley of Littondale. Of the wealth of attractive villages, Linton, Burnsall and Arncliffe rank superlatives, while the Dales Way stamps its approval by opting to trace the Wharfe for more than thirty miles from Ilkley to its birth in the wilderness of Langstrothdale, beyond Buckden.

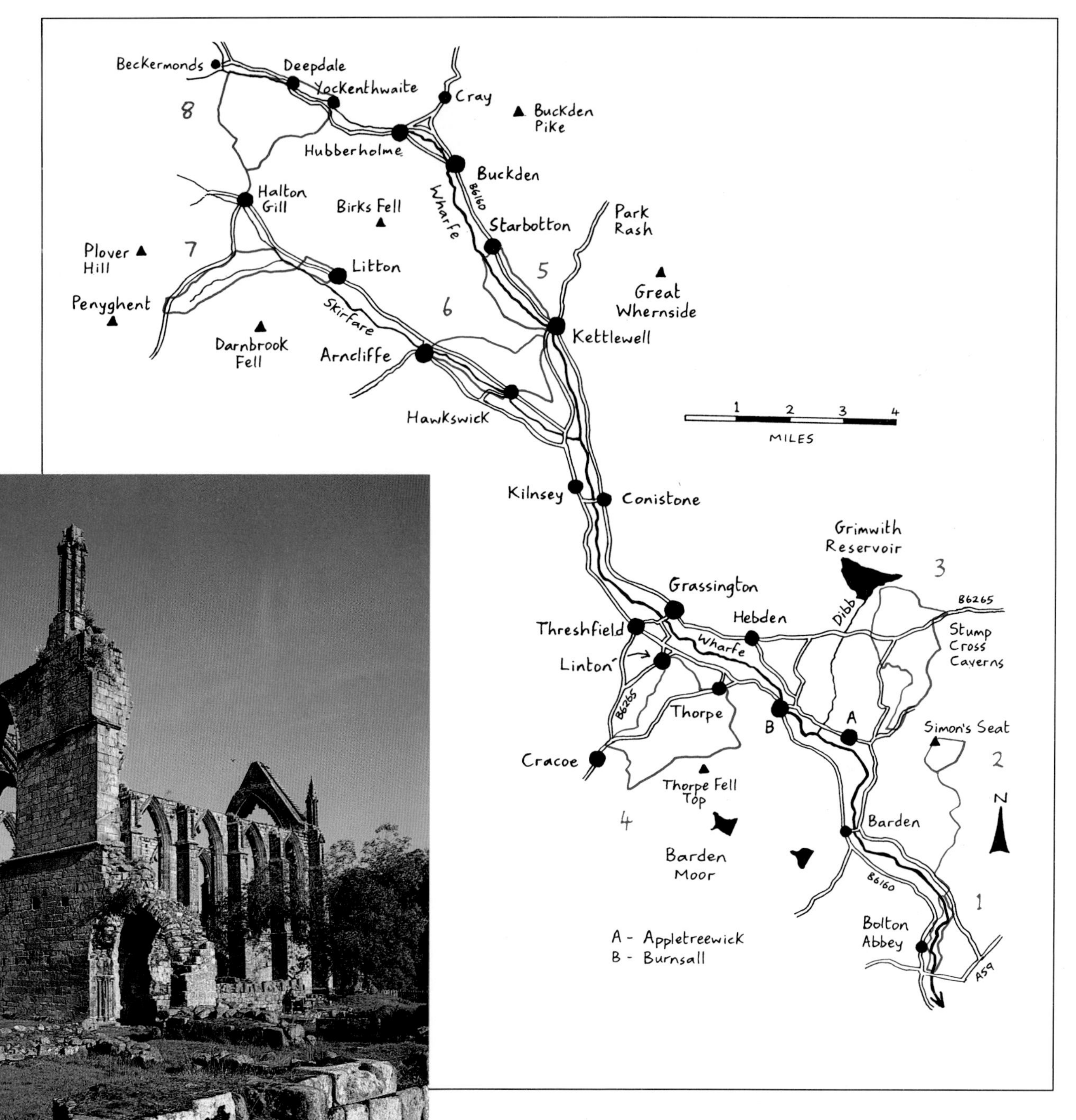

Bolton Priory

1: THE WHARFE AT BOLTON ABBEY

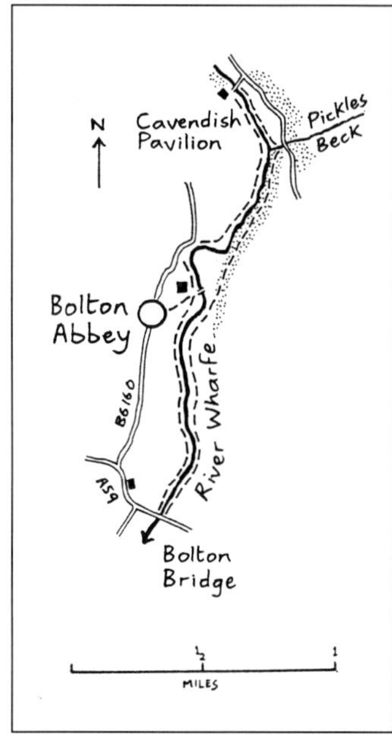

The Wharfe swings round to approach Bolton Priory

Start:
Bolton Abbey (Cavendish Pavilion)

Distance:
4½ miles

Map:
1:25,000 - Yorkshire Dales South
1:50,000 - Landranger 104

There is not a great deal that hasn't already been said about Bolton Abbey, though the most useful information is the advice to avoid it during the height of summer. This has been a hugely popular destination for generations of trippers, the authentic approach being by wagonette from the old railway station. It was the station, incidentally, that gave the name Bolton Abbey to the village, for the stately ruin is properly the priory.

This uncomplicated walk patrols both banks of the Wharfe between the Pavilion at the entrance to Strid Wood, and Bolton Bridge, where it glides out of the National Park. Leaving the café along the strath of Sand Holme - which will be one vast car park if earlier advice has not been heeded - the priory is soon espied to good advantage. The Augustinian canons of Embsay made a wise judgement call when presented with the chance to move the few miles here in 1151.

While a flat pasture by a river may be a typical abbey site, it is the crowding in of the high moors that places Bolton Priory in a setting of unsurpassed beauty. The one stroke of fortune at the Dissolution was the sparing of the nave, to function to this day as the parish church. The west tower fared less well, though stone plundering and the ravages of the centuries can't be held entirely responsible - it was still in the midst of construction in 1536 when this idyllic set-up came to an abrupt end. Alongside in these capacious park-like grounds is Bolton Hall, long-time shooting lodge of the Duke of Devonshire.

The Wharfe at Bolton Bridge

The Priory from the wooded heights across the Wharfe

Morning light over the Wharfe at Bolton Bridge, looking to Beamsley Beacon

The return walk to Bolton Bridge is a tranquil wander, and here at least there is a guarantee of some peace. Waggons rumbling over the old bridge are neatly avoided by a hidden footbridge, across which there is immediate re-engagement with the Wharfe. Survivors of unsavoury scenes at Red Lion Farm will be relieved to discover that the right of way has finally been diverted to safer ground alongside. A special moment arrives when level with the priory again, for it is now revealed while gazing down from a dramatic coign of vantage. The walk's final quarter brings a pleasant change, being largely wooded and, initially, retaining height advantage above the river.

Now, if the parking fee didn't put you in the red, a can of pop at the Pavilion might finish you off!

2: THE ASCENT OF SIMON'S SEAT

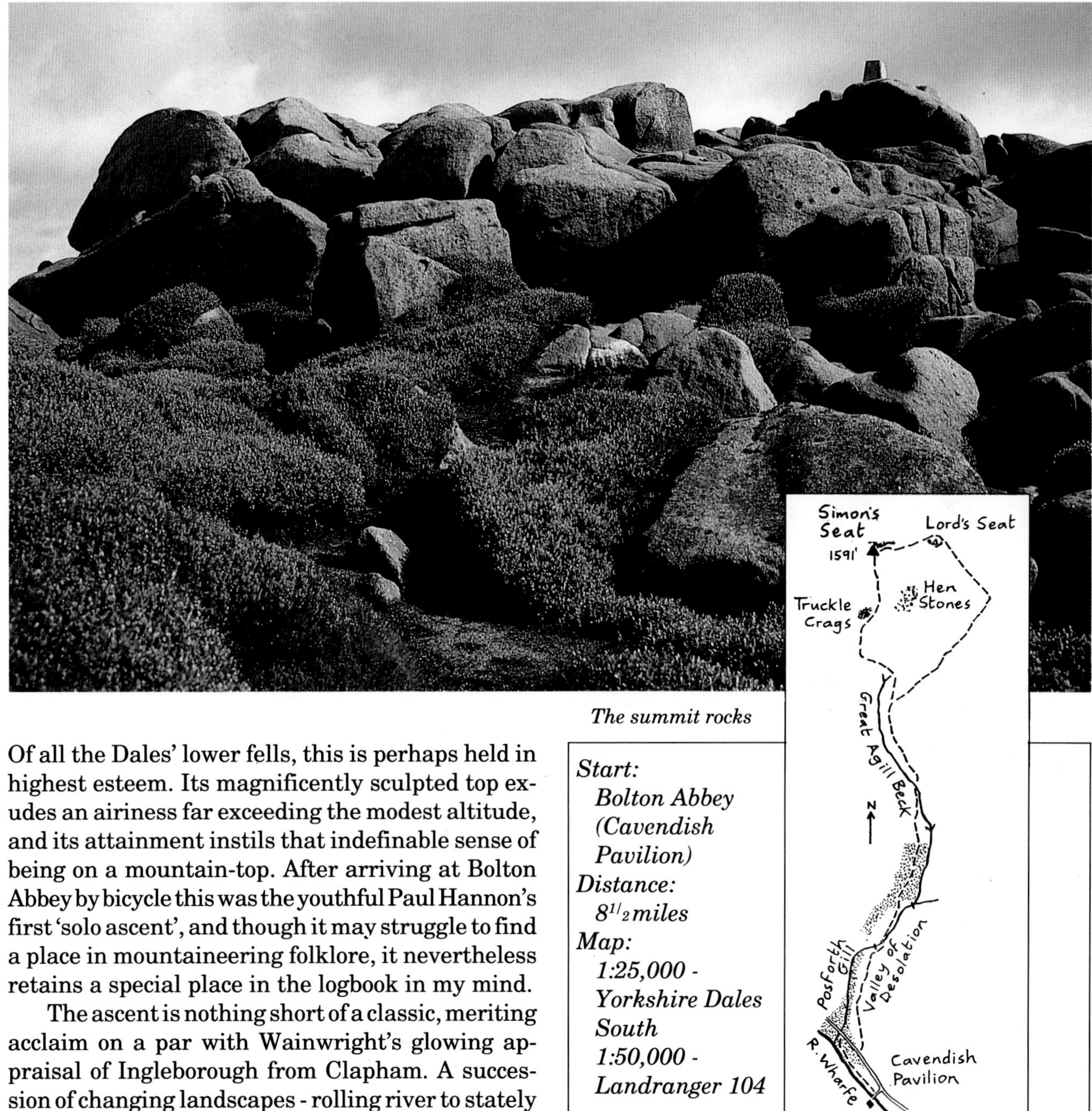

The summit rocks

Start:
Bolton Abbey (Cavendish Pavilion)
Distance:
$8^{1/2}$ miles
Map:
1:25,000 - Yorkshire Dales South
1:50,000 - Landranger 104

Of all the Dales' lower fells, this is perhaps held in highest esteem. Its magnificently sculpted top exudes an airiness far exceeding the modest altitude, and its attainment instils that indefinable sense of being on a mountain-top. After arriving at Bolton Abbey by bicycle this was the youthful Paul Hannon's first 'solo ascent', and though it may struggle to find a place in mountaineering folklore, it nevertheless retains a special place in the logbook in my mind.

The ascent is nothing short of a classic, meriting acclaim on a par with Wainwright's glowing appraisal of Ingleborough from Clapham. A succession of changing landscapes - rolling river to stately parkland to tumbling beck to silent forest to breezy

moorland to the ultimate crown, a rock-girt summit. From the Pavilion bridge you are soon strolling eagerly past gnarled oaks en route to Posforth Gill, where the Valley of Desolation has clearly made a complete recovery from the violent storms that christened it over a hundred and fifty years ago. Two very different but engaging waterfalls await inspection, the main one below the path, with the upper waterslide a short way up a minor diversion.

A plantation cushions this low country from the expansive moorland acres, and once in the open a glorious stroll up a sandy track brings first the outcrops of Truckle Crags and then the summit rocks into sight. Resembling a toddler's brick building exercise, the tumble of boulders cause eager anticipation, and one must have long ceased to be young at heart to ignore their call to be explored. Indeed, a modest scramble is needed if only to claim the summit. While a ubiquitous Ordnance column may be the sole point of interest on many a Pennine top, that cemented onto Simon's Seat's platform is shamed by the mass of gritstone around. The icing on the cake of this approach is that the final moment of glory is saved until literally that last step: only from the ultimate perch do you gain the remarkable bird's-eye view over Skyreholme, with Trollers Gill prominent.

Reversal of the outward route is, for once, wholeheartedly recommended, though it can be varied initially by taking in a visit to Lord's Seat, which lends itself to further scrambling games before tracks filter back to the main route. If a change is demanded, then seek out a path striking west to the moor-edge above Howgill, to plunge through forestry to the Wharfe, whose bank leads unfailingly back by way of Barden Bridge and Strid Wood.

top:
Waterslide at the upper falls, Posforth Gill

bottom:
Heavy traffic fording Great Agill Beck

3: GRIMWITH AND TROLLERS GILL

Start:
Stump Cross Caverns
Distance:
$7^{1}/_{2}$ miles
Map:
1:25,000 - Yorkshire Dales South
1:50,000 - Landranger 99

Walkers on Nursery Knot pause to survey the Skyreholme scene, with Black Hill Road leading the eye to Simon's Seat

The side-valley of Skyreholme cradles a wealth of interest in the lap of Simon's Seat and the wind-swept Craven Moor. Although Skyreholme itself makes a natural starting point, lay-bys near Stump Cross are also well placed. Stump Cross Caverns is a show-cave of many years' standing, and promises a rewarding experience, possibly at the end of the walk. In the passages beneath our feet are a host of weird and wonderful rock formations, perfect for those of us intrigued by the great underworld but lacking the loose slate to venture where real cavers go.

Back in the open air meanwhile, a start that could not contrast more with the darkness below sets off overland, first stop being the limestone tor of Nursery Knot, summit of the walk even at this early stage. On view are Grimwith's chilly waters backed by slopes eventually terminating in Great Whernside, with the dark wall of Simon's Seat filling a circle of sombre uplands. Unkempt pastures lead to the reservoir, much enlarged and now a habitat of watersport types. Unless adding four miles by encircling the lake, only a short length of its shore is followed around to the keepers' houses and car park. A handsome track climbs away over high ground, offering extensive views over Wharfedale to Barden Moor. Across the Pateley road a more sumptuous green way takes the reins to approach the neighbourhood of Trollers Gill.

To gain the secretive head of the gill the pothole of Hell Hole is passed en route to a miner's track: this runs down through old lead workings to omit Trollers Gill, but most walkers choose the scintillating route through the ravine. Hidden behind Middle Hill, only a slender trod gives away the half-minute crossing at its neck to reveal the upper reaches of the limestone gorge. An unexpectedly easy passage through its dry bed, with bare walls spawning scree and sparse vegetation, ends abruptly at the entrance. After giving thanks for being saved from the clutches of its occupant 'Barguest' the spectral hound, the definitive path is regained at the nab end of Middle Hill.

Bowery Skyreholme Beck leads by a long-burst dam to its sparse hamlet. Hidden in trees across the beck is the part-Elizabethan Parceval Hall, a retreat centre with attractive grounds open to the public. A climb up Skyreholme Bank leaves one wondering why the traffic-free road is so well surfaced, after which the green carpet of Black Hill Road affords open views over the country traversed. On meeting the road at Dry Gill, the promise of teas offers a final aside in this walk of many distractions.

The inviting green track linking Grimwith and Trollers Gill

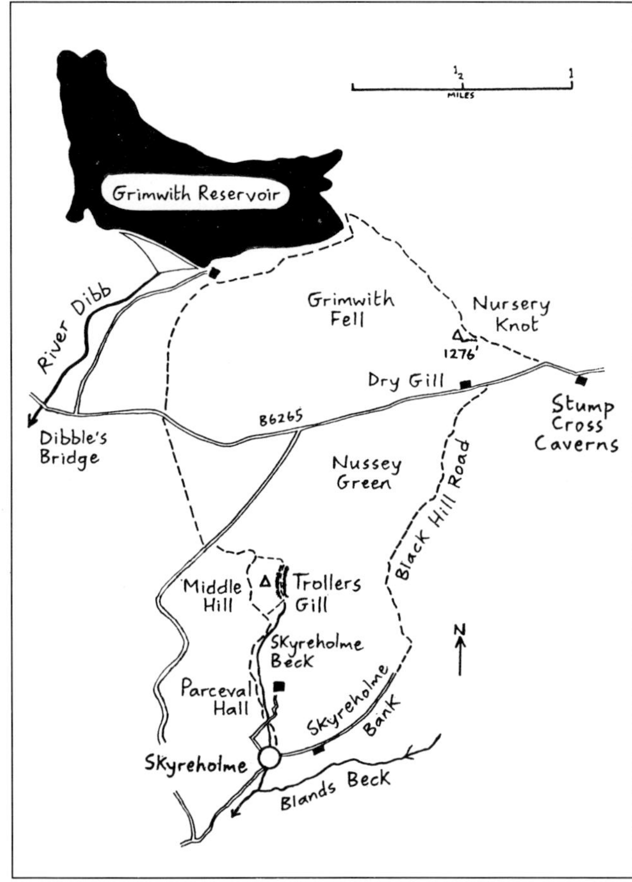

The forbidding entrance to Trollers Gill

Simon's Seat over Middle Hill from above the old lead mine

4: THORPE FELL AND CRACOE FELL

Summer storm clouds envelope the heart of the dale, as seen from the Thorpe Fell edges

Start:
Linton
Distance:
9 miles
Map:
1:25,000 - Yorkshire Dales South
1:50,000 - Landranger 98 & 103

Even a walker largely ignorant of his surroundings cannot fail to be aware of the successful Dales' partnership of limestone and gritstone, and this walk extends equal billing to the twosome. Emerald fields parcelled by white walls are brooded over by dark moorland on its millstone grit bed, the two sections linked by a brace of identical lanes acting as corridors between village and moor.

Linton-in-Craven's charms are simply irrepressible: within the space of a few yards its tiny beck is spanned by packhorse, road and clapper bridges alongside stepping-stones and a ford, all watched over by a sloping green, a whitewashed inn and the Fountaine Hospital almshouses dating from 1721. While Linton may have its share of pretty village awards, when the moors beckon, there's only one winner. Key to the hills is Thorpe-in-the-Hollow (another Sunday name), reached by way of fields and a narrow lane that still finds room for a central reservation. Reposing snugly in the folds of reef knolls, Thorpe is said to have proven elusive to the plundering Scots, and its seclusion has ensured much the same anonymity ever since.

At the terminus of the spidery fell lane, Barden Moor lays a sunken carpet to set a course over its heathery floor. The deep grooves are a legacy of this old way's origin, for bringing sleds of peat or coal

right: Approaching the monument on Cracoe Fell

Cracoe Fell and monument from the foot of the fell lane

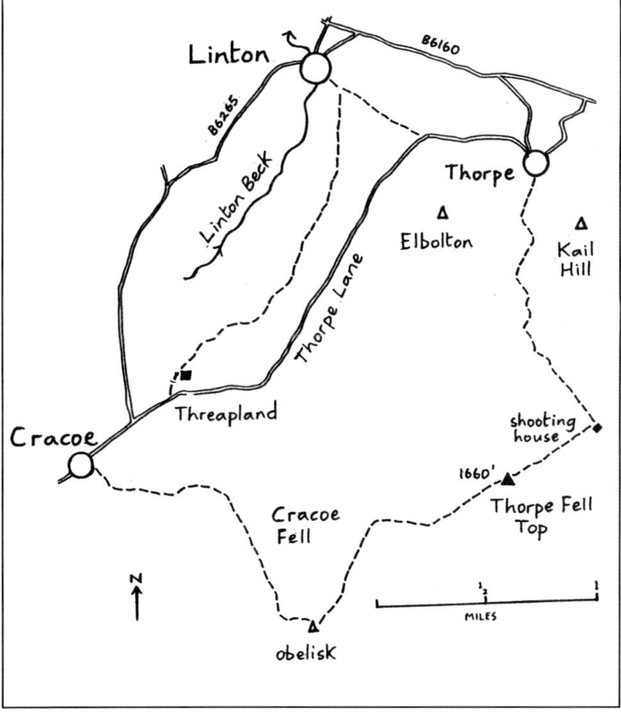

down from the tops. A shooting house stands waiting, and while Land-Rover tracks abound, none prove suitable for the purpose of locating Thorpe Fell Top, crown of Barden Moor. Free-ranging through heather is the order of the day, the unchained hiker's epitome of rambling, and tolerable to most walkers if not limitless: in the rough grass and tussocky heather, Linton's orderly oasis is a lifetime away.

At 1660ft the Ordnance column keeps guard over a wide sweep of moor, with Dales' features restricted to distant horizons. Also claiming the skyline is the obelisk on Cracoe Fell, a sure guide to playing out the second half of this rough-stuff. Cracoe's war victims are remembered on this strategic perch, a prominent landmark to travellers on the road at the base of the fell. It is built fair and square onto a gritstone plinth, the most obvious halting place on the walk.

Cracoe is a toy village far below, and the way thereto homes in on the head of its fell lane. Clattering quarry waggons on the road that splits Cracoe make for a return with mixed feelings to civilisation, and though they are soon left behind, there is more devastation to come. From the farm at Threapland a mile and a half of restful pastures conclude the walk, the one (and in this case one's enough) jarring note is the source of many of those waggons, the bellowing quarry that smears dust indiscriminately over its muted surroundings.

Right: The packhorse bridge at Linton

Descending one of the old quarry tracks on Cracoe Fell, with the Craven lowlands outstretched below

5: ABOVE THE WHARFE TO STARBOTTON

The departure of the last Ice Age left the upper reaches of Wharfedale in an uncomplicated shape, and I set out on this excursion to be perfectly placed to appraise the result. A glance at the layout hereabouts makes it blindly obvious that if you leave the riverbank you are destined for a fair degree of work, but on this occasion my chosen route declined to climb to the surrounding ridge-lines, and the benefits of an access track ensured the gradients couldn't ask too much either.

The whole of Kettlewell's maze of dwellings occupy the east bank of the river, so after donning woolly headgear to combat the stinging February winds, first task was to cross the Wharfe to begin the climb to Moor End. This defunct farmhouse - now an outdoor pursuits centre - must have always proven a struggle to run up here at 1225ft, though its setting is truly magnificent. Only a handful of level pastures gave chance to soak up the surround

Looking back to Kettlewell from Moor End

Start:
Kettlewell
Distance:
5 miles
Map:
1:25,000 - Yorkshire Dales North / Central
1:50,000 - Landranger 98

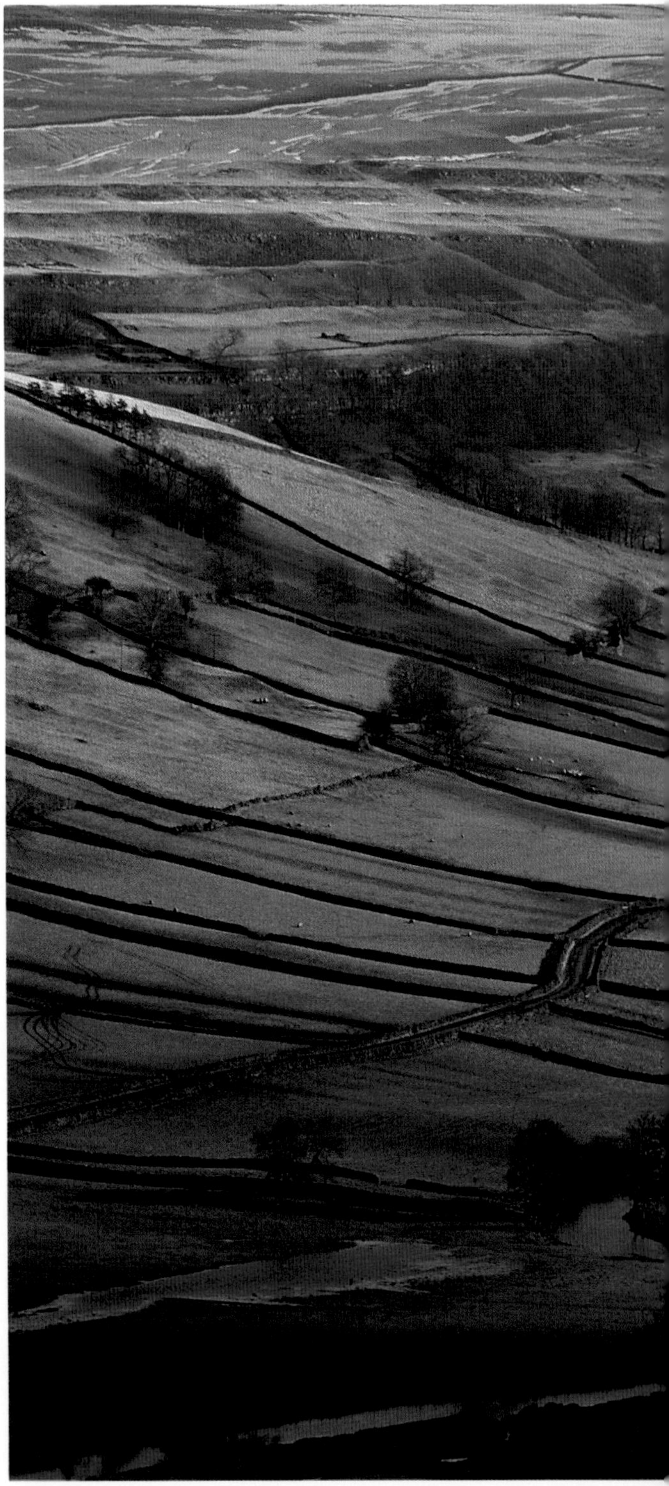

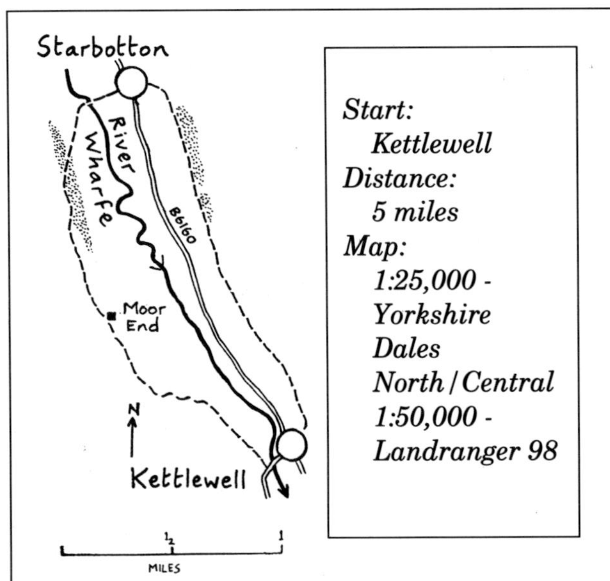

of high country before I started back for the valley, but the frenetic clouds chose this elevated half hour to inflict a salvo of wintry assaults on me and, apparently, me alone. From the cleanly-draped mountains of the dalehead etched against a blue sky I would find even the walls in front of me suddenly vanish.

The sluggish meanderings of the Wharfe gave much interest in addition to admiring the situation of my goal, the village of Starbotton beneath the massive sprawl of Buckden Pike. Descent was through a hoary old wood, on an inter-valley track crossing the moor from Arncliffe - just one section of one of the old drove routes that criss-cross the Dales. A pointer to its age is found in the final sunken section before the river.

Starbotton was to provide the only life I would encounter, and as such merited a potter round its seductive back lanes to seek out the tiny plot of an old Quaker burial ground. The return to Kettlewell down the east side of the valley neatly paralleled the outward section without attempting to mirror it. This was also part of the plan, for only a field's length above the road, it was sufficient both to escape the traffic and survey that outward route, yet asked nothing strenuous of me in return.

opposite: Buckden Pike and Starbotton from near Moor End
left: Cottages at Starbotton
above: On the Wharfe's bank
below: Wharfedale at Starbotton

6: BETWEEN SKIRFARE AND WHARFE

At the little known confluence of Amerdale Dub near Kilnsey, the river Skirfare is absorbed by the Wharfe: in the preceding miles they have travelled a near-identical course, and this jaunt has been planned to witness their journeys in equal proportion. Though Arncliffe is a charming place to end a walk, Kettlewell may be seen as a more logical start, enabling the valley section to be slotted in between two climbs. Dividing these dales is the great wedge of moorland that labours its way up to all but the 2000ft mark on Birks Fell, and of the half-dozen recognised crossings, this walk utilises the first and lowest pair, over Hawkswick and Old Cote Moors.

The only exertions are faced in the first half-mile, during a climb to Byre Bank Wood tucked beneath the ledge of Park Scar. Steadier stuff covers the rise to the crest at 1600ft on the ridge, and ahead now Wharfedale steals the show, with Buckden Pike filling the frame. As height is lost a

Looking across to Kettlewell and Great Whernside from Old Cote Moor

The Littondale landscape

more intimate scene builds up, and the aptly named Slit shoe-horns walkers down through a scar to enjoy a bird's-eye view of Kettlewell. This sizeable community that once survived largely on lead mining is now equally dependant on the tourist industry, and though the owners of most of the cottages may flaunt an affluence unknown to their earlier occupants, from our lofty and naive perch, at least, little appears to have altered.

Whether breaking or ending a journey, Kettlewell always merits a stroll round its network of lanes, though a direct return to Littondale need not cross the Wharfe. From the Kilnsey road the lower level inter-valley path quickly regains the ridge-wall under Hawkswick Moor, its views dominated by limestone in the terraces above Conistone and the shadowy neighbourhood of Kilnsey Crag. In the image of its ascent the path slants towards slumbering Hawkswick, stealing through unnoticed to find the Skirfare. Though the river is hardly a constant companion, its adjacent pastures guide back to Arncliffe in leisurely fashion - the only way to go in Littondale.

top: Walkers from Kettlewell climb to the Slit

bottom: The sequestered charm of St. Oswald's, Arncliffe

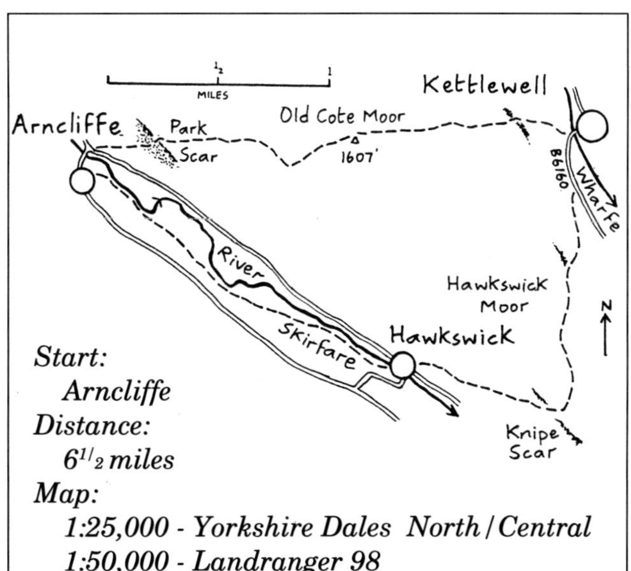

In the final stages the Skirfare is less elusive as it returns to a corner of the village where the grey church of St. Oswald squints through trees into the waters mirroring the bridge. The house across the bridge was a port of call for Charles Kingsley when staying at Malham Tarn House, while a house facing the green is a haven for thirsty walkers converging here from any number of tracks over the hills. Refreshment that finds its way to the glass by way of barrel and jug is a tradition very appropriate to Arncliffe's timeless qualities.

above:
Arncliffe shelters beneath Old Cote Moor

right:
The heart of Kettlewell

7: AROUND PENYGHENT GILL

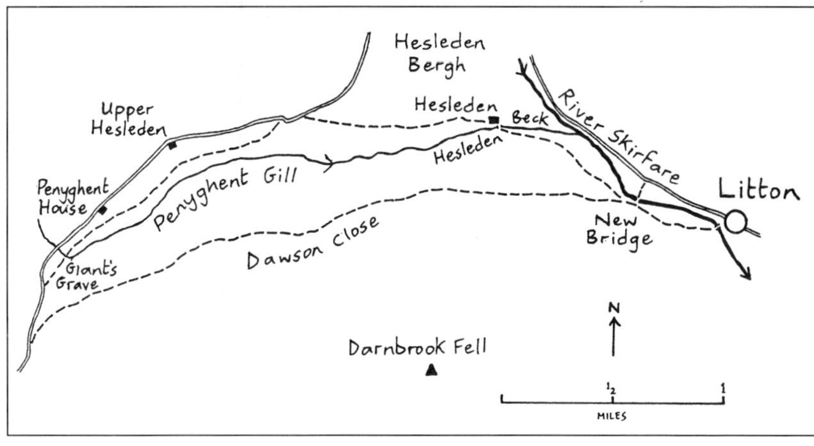

A walker on Hesleden Bergh looks across Littondale to the bulky wall of Horse Head

Start:
Litton
Distance:
8 miles
Map:
1:25,000 - Yorkshire Dales North / Central
1:50,000 - Landranger 98

Everyone with a pair of boots knows of Penyghent, but only a few will be familiar with the beck that claims that name. Being destined for the Wharfe - in preference to the Ribble with which the mountain is associated - has helped preserve the beck's anonymity, coupled with the fact that it chooses to burrow underground as often as it can. This elongated horseshoe hitherto revealed surprisingly little of its tinkling waters until a welcome footpath creation traded a mile of road walking for a spectacular promenade above the gill's upper reaches.

Litton is scattered casually along the valley road, the cluster of dwellings at its western end being key to a footbridge over the often dry Skirfare. Further updale the start of the old road to Stainforth is met at New Bridge: mercifully left to stay green, it is now destined to guide, in due course, all the way back. For now settle for continuing updale to Hesleden, where beyond the yapping farm dogs a path breasts Hesleden Bergh to connect with the modern Stainforth road out of Halton Gill. Almost at once the new path makes itself available for that walk along the rim of the gill, a mile and a half of Dales' magic with waterplay, miniature ravines, and scars in profusion. The road is met again at the barely evident giant's grave where it crosses the gill fresh from its moorland seepings. Penyghent, meanwhile, lends a profile known only to its devotees.

top: Deep inside Penyghent Gill
bottom: Warm evening light on Litton's Queen's Arms

overleaf (page 36): Penyghent from the infant Penyghent Gill

Yet again tarmac is underfoot for yards only before a 'no through road' sign encourages a doubling back to commence the glorious return. This unblemished green road runs the flanks of Darnbrook Fell and provides outstanding views to the head of Littondale. For fully three miles it is yours to savour, and arrival at New Bridge leaves a rich feeling of satisfaction. Thank the Almighty that not all these highways fell victim to modern road builders!

The Skirfare at Litton
. . . . . and (right) during a drier spell

8: ACROSS HORSE HEAD RIDGE

Start:
Halton Gill
Distance:
8 miles
Map:
1:25,000 - Yorkshire Dales North / Central
1:50,000 - Landranger 98

Yockenthwaite Stone Circle

Halton Gill is springboard to a relatively demanding foray utilising the two highest level tracks linking Littondale with Langstrothdale in upper Wharfedale, though if the larks are singing their summer tunes it won't be a step too long. The two paths on offer can hardly be termed passes, for the broad Horse Head-Birks Fell ridge offers no such openings - when you come over here, you come over the top. A crucial feature of the walk is the two miles of riverside walking that not only contrast starkly with the open moorland, but also exert a calming influence when inserted between those windswept heights.

The outward leg is the better known, clearer, and less taxing of the two, for the climb over Horse Head Gate takes a dignified track once frequented by the incumbent of Halton Gill, who would ride or walk over to take service at Hubberholme. Surely he also would take great delight in his surroundings, and seek out the distinct outlines of the two shapeliest Dales' mountains Ingleborough and Penyghent as they entered the frame. A less well made green path is the escort down the moor to

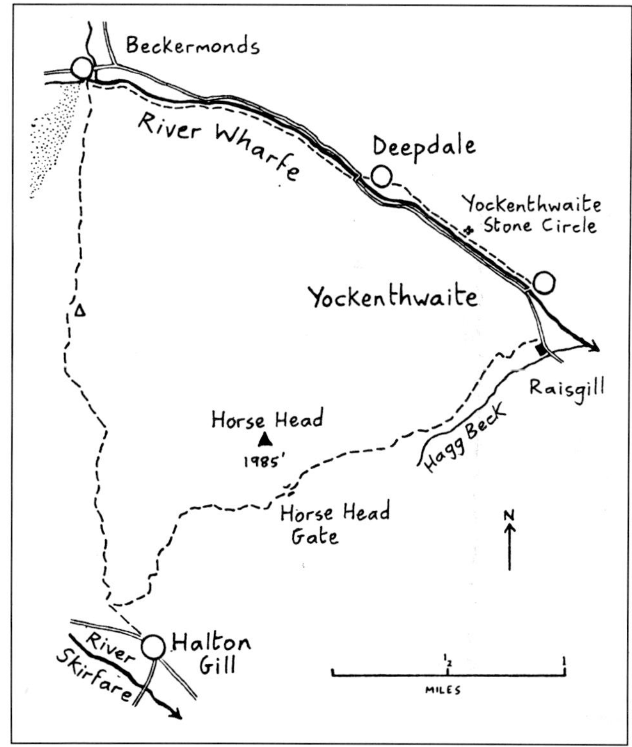

Hagg Gill, whose welcome colour is a foretaste of the Wharfe's own banks.

Yockenthwaite, Deepdale and Beckermonds are uniformly spaced farm communities from which the sounds of school bell and chinking ale-glass have long departed down-dale. This walk's entire patronage of the Wharfe is well-favoured in occupying the opposite bank to the road, and the chief feature of interest - aside from ravaging natural beauty - also sits on the right bank for the walker. Yockenthwaite's stone circle may have no pretensions to the scale of Stonehenge, but its compact grouping makes an inspiring contribution to the scene.

Last duty in the valley is to witness the birth of the Wharfe as Greenfield and Oughtershaw becks merge, then it's shoulders to the wheel to face the ever-upward trudge to the ridge-top. A stone man signals the end of the pull, a lone figure who still pines for a partner that clearly once shared his skilfully constructed platform. The illustrious Three Peaks return to the fray on the descent, with the path's sketchy moments aided by the occasional stile and marker post. A bird's-eye view of Halton Gill adds a late flourish to the closing stages of this invigorating tramp.

above: *The youthful Wharfe tumbles through Langstrothdale*
below: *Dales Wayfarers on the Wharfeside path above Yockenthwaite*
opposite top: *On the crest of Horse Head, looking back to a triumvirate of Craven mountains - Fountains Fell, Penyghent and Plover Hill*
opposite bottom: *Horse Head ridge and Greenfield Beck from above Beckermonds on an autumn evening*

CHAPTER TWO MALHAMDALE

WALK 9 CROOKRISE CRAG & EMBSAY MOOR 42

WALK 10 THE HEART OF MALHAMDALE 46

WALK 11 PIKEDAW & MALHAM COVE 49

WALK 12 GORDALE SCAR & MASTILES LANE 53

WALK 13 AROUND MALHAM MOOR 57

Unlike its string of easterly flowing colleagues, the river Aire is given short thrift by the Dales, and soon finds itself sullied by a succession of industrial towns. Linked in perpetuity with the Aire is its birthplace Malham, and if this river had nothing else to offer, it would earn acclaim enough for its exploits in its limestone beginnings above this revered village. By common consent this heart of the Craven Dales has been adopted as Malhamdale as far down the valley as its gateway of Gargrave. Scattered above the Aire's banks are a number of villages that happily accept their subservience to tiny Malham, a veritable nerve centre of operations. In sight of the village, and much of the valley for that matter, is the bold face of Malham Cove, while tucked away between enveloping hills is the great cleft of its partner Gordale Scar. On the breezy heights above this famous twosome are found Malham Tarn and Moor, and their many attendant features of this outstanding limestone district.

There is more to Malhamdale than limestone's gleaming magnificence however, and what gives the area its startling contrast is the country east of the Aire, where a medley of innocuous becks drain what is typical gritstone country. The moors above Hetton and Winterburn play support to the great mass of Barden Moor, of sufficient girth to divide its duties between Wharfedale and the Aire country. Gritstone escarpments, heather moors and bracken slopes forge a landscape that gives Malhamdale breadth as well as diversity.

Mastiles Lane rolls on over its upland course

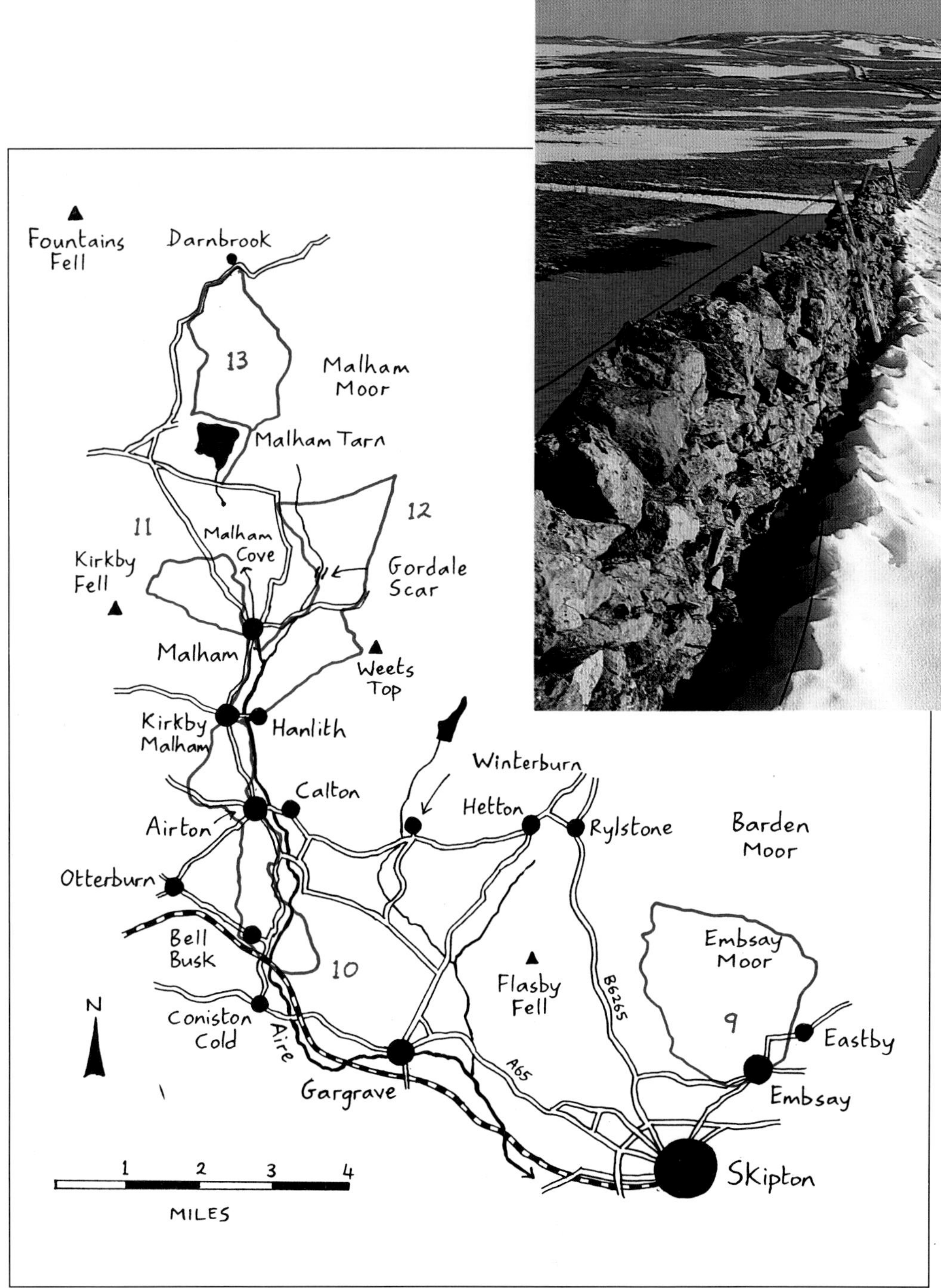

9: CROOKRISE CRAG AND EMBSAY MOOR

Start:
Embsay
Distance:
8 miles
Map:
1:25,000 -
Yorkshire Dales South
1:50,000 -
Landranger 103 & 104

right: *A view to savour - on the brow of Crookrise*

below: *The snow-capped Malhamdale hills from the gritstone of Crookrise Crag*

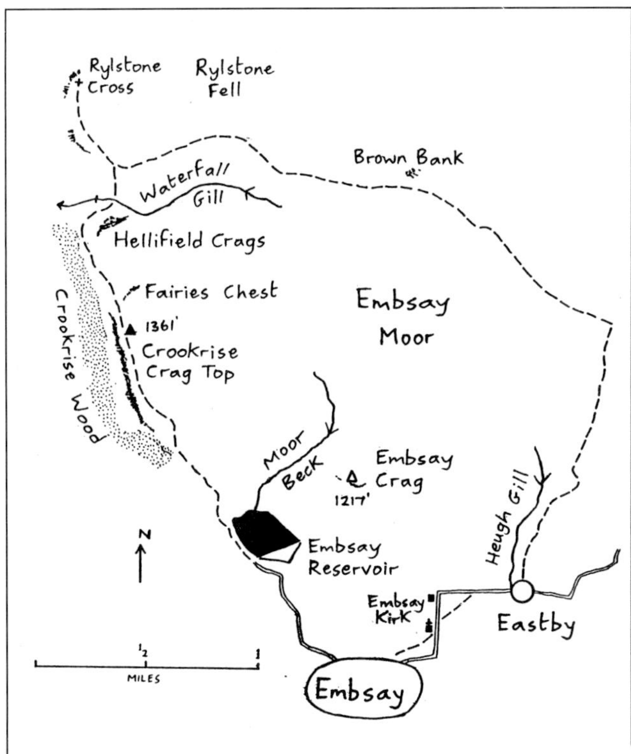

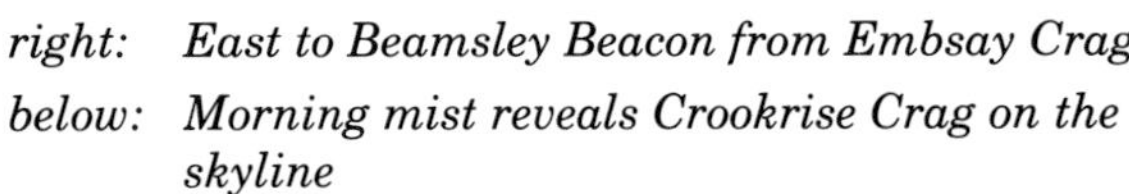
right: *East to Beamsley Beacon from Embsay Crag*
below: *Morning mist reveals Crookrise Crag on the skyline*

The climbers' playground of Crookrise is also a prized objective of the rambler, who will thrive on an unhurried promenade along the crest of this revered gritstone escarpment.

Departing the village by way of a mill pond alive with ducks, the road to the hills grants an unrivalled prospect of the prow of Embsay Crag across the chilly waters of the reservoir. An archetypal gritstone path mounts the moor edge, and on the brow a thoughtfully placed stile transfers us to the dramatic side of the wall to wring every drop of pleasure out of the walk to the Ordnance column. Beneath our feet, shattered rocks secreting a hundred howfs tumble through the bracken to plantations that do little to mar the scene: Crookrise Crag Top is not a place to pass, it's a place to halt and savour.

When the time to leave does arrive, it's back onto the moor to continue past the outcrops of Fairies Chest to the greater formations of Hellifield Crag. Although Waterfall Gill is crossed here, its principal feature, a little downstream, is easily missed. Just a short climb further encounters the only track traversing the moor that can be enjoyed on any day of the year. This is the Rylstone-Bolton Abbey bridleway, more romantically dubbed the White Doe track after immortalisation by Wordsworth in his tale of the ill-fated Nortons of Rylstone.

The way of the White Doe is ours too, though from this point a detour might be made to the landmark of Rylstone Cross, another short climb further along the escarpment. The bridleway, meanwhile, produces a stirring march into the heart of this moorland dome. The undulating acres of Embsay Moor give the lungs a complete re-bore, with the only interruptions being the merging with a shooters' track above a brace of ling-roofed huts, a scattering of boulders on the walk's high point, and a guidepost signalling a speedier return to Embsay Kirk.

Striding on, however, a further mile is knocked off before the next guidepost sends an intermittent way running past shooting houses and grouse butts to Eastby Gate. Bidding farewell to the moor which has for so long absorbed us, an improving path drops through the pastures to Embsay's kid brother Eastby. A useful field-path shortcuts the road to pass Embsay's church en route to a stile into the car park to score a bullseye finish.

The miniature peak of Sharp Haw leads the eye to distant Pendle Hill beyond the Aire Gap, as seen from Crookrise Crag Top

Looking back to Embsay Crag from the climb to Crookrise

10: THE HEART OF MALHAMDALE

Unfashionable Bell Busk may seem an unlikely springboard for the 'heart of Malhamdale', but in practice it is well sited for an updale ramble in which the Aire links two attractive villages set above its bank. The midway pivot of Airton is also well sited to enable the walk to be split down the middle.

Tucked away from the A65 at Coniston Cold, Bell Busk spreads below the Skipton-Settle railway where a low viaduct grubs across the Aire. Taking to the old road to Gargrave from the confluence with Otterburn Beck, Haw Crag assumes an aggressive profile high above. Crowned by an Ordnance column, at a mere 676ft it serves as a fine Malhamdale viewpoint, with greatest interest being in the sighting of the Cove.

Oblivious to this craggy scene the Pennine Way runs only a field's length to the east, to descend unmoorlike Eshton Moor to greet the Aire again. This time keep faith with this most unassuming of rivers through the soothing pastures to Airton, with only Newfield Bridge interrupting proceedings. Airton's own bridge sits in the shadow of an old cotton mill, externally unharmed by conversion to flats. Now a path on the mill bank proffers more interest in the form of its defunct mill-race, which parallels the river and sandwiches the path into a double waterside walk. A footbridge resumes the going on the east bank, through park-like grounds to the final bridge at Hanlith.

opposite: *Pennine Wayfarers at Airton Mill*

above: *The Aire at Newfield Bridge*

right: *The attractive facade of the old vicarage, Kirkby Malham*

Start:
Bell Busk
Distance:
9 miles
Map:
1:25,000 - Yorkshire Dales South
1:50,000 - Landranger 98 & 103

Hanlith Bridge

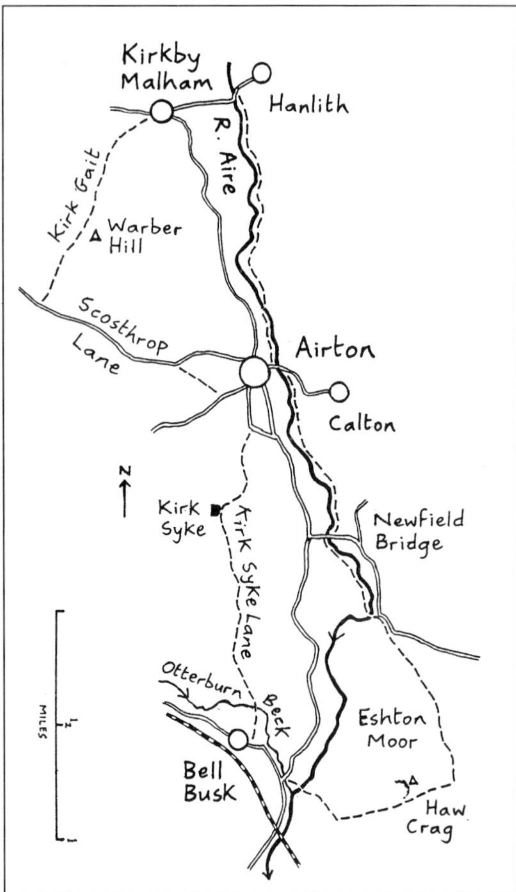

Up the lane is Kirkby Malham, its amply proportioned church celebrating both its half-millennium in 1990 and Oliver Cromwell's signature in the register. This shady corner is left by a discreet footbridge at the end of Kirk Gait, a route known by generations of church-bound Otterburn residents. A stiff pull onto Warber Hill earns a structured view of the dale before running along to Scosthrop Lane and down to Airton.

Though larger than its neighbours Airton possesses neither shop nor hostelry, and if detouring to its green, one is left to stare at the 'squatter's house', an island dwelling that in times past housed local down-and-outs. In these 'property boom' days there are no doubt many who would relish the chance of setting up home in this highly individual dwelling, regardless of its history! The final stage sees further churchgoing connections paving the way for a march along generally green and pleasant Kirk Syke Lane, bound unerringly for Bell Busk.

11: PIKEDAW AND MALHAM COVE

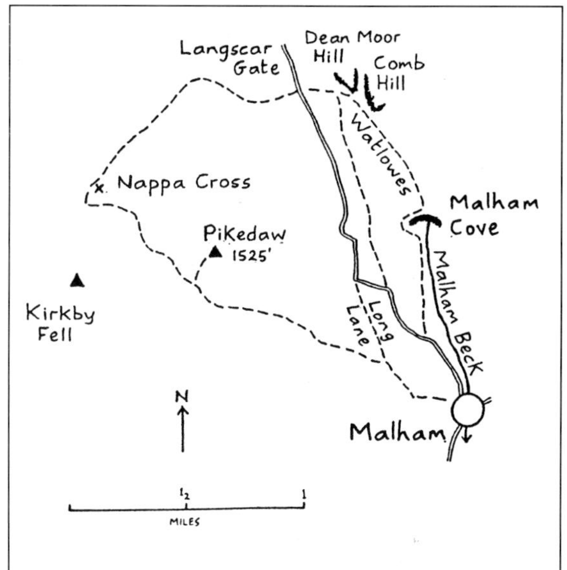

Not all walks from Malham need be dogged by the bustling crowds, and this exercise is a prime example of what can be achieved.

Leaving those crowds behind within yards of the overflowing car park, farm lanes usher you out past field barns for which Ordnance Surveyors have diligently researched individual names. Above them a smashing path climbs between limestone scars and a tiny beck which denotes the line of the Mid Craven Fault. Allegiance to limestone repays with a clamber to the cairned crest of Pikedaw for a deserved sojourn upon this prized Malhamdale viewpoint. On regaining the path, easier slopes lead past the shaft of a former calamine pit and over a limestone pavement to meet the Settle-Malham bridleway. With the dome of Kirkby Fell watching over, the bridleway is departed at a junction from

above: Nappa Cross and a distant Malham Tarn

left: A decorated cave entrance above Pikedaw

where the restored shaft of the old guidepost of Nappa Cross points the way for a superior green track to work its way down to the Malham Moor road at Langscar Gate.

Down the field rise the statuesque tors of Dean Moor Hill and Comb Hill, craggy sentinels of Watlowes, the Dry Valley. Here the option is to save the Cove and the limestone features above it for another walk, or to succumb to its undeniably greater attraction and head down the Dry Valley.

Crisp snows demote the gleaming limestone of the Cove into drab grey

Watlowes plants you fair and square on the great limestone pavement on top of the Cove, and while the deep grikes secrete timid ferns and flowers, they are also poised to ensnare wayward steps. It will of course be readily acknowledged that extreme caution is required if peering over the alarming precipice. The sheer 300ft face will be revealed in all its glory on descending the staircase down the side to the issuing Malham Beck, to meet the tourist route back to the village.

To maintain the nature of the walk an alternative avoids the blatant temptations of Cove country, and rather than dropping into the Dry Valley,

traces a route through a string of stiles parallel with the road. The green course of Long Lane, initially unenclosed, can be used to re-enter Malham again by the back door, to ask 'crowds, what crowds?'

Start:	*Malham*
Distance:	*5½ miles*
Map:	*1:25,000 - Yorkshire Dales South*
	1:50,000 - Landranger 98

below: *Malham Beck leading the eye to the village from the rim of the Cove*

overleaf: *At Malham Cove*

12: GORDALE SCAR AND MASTILES LANE

Looking out from the portals of Gordale Scar

In considering the primeval savagery of Gordale Scar to upstage the mighty Cove itself, I am certainly not alone: its sinister form enhances its appeal to the selfish walker, for the prospect of a scramble in the Scar's innermost confines deters the casual visitor from onward progress.

I left Malham to trace the beck downstream, and was quickly lured by a branch path to the charms of Gordale Beck. Though short-lived, an engaging pocket of woodland served as a fitting introduction to the ever-lovely Janet's Foss. True to form, the fairy queen failed to emerge from behind her waterfall, but as always I set aside a few quiet moments in this dreamy dell, just in case.

No sooner was Janet out of my mind then Gordale Scar muscled its way in, as an incongruous campsite led to the limestone bastions that often as not shun their dazzling reputation to appear dark and forbidding. Only on entering the inner sanctum was the full splendour of the scene revealed, as a twist in

Upper falls, Gordale Scar

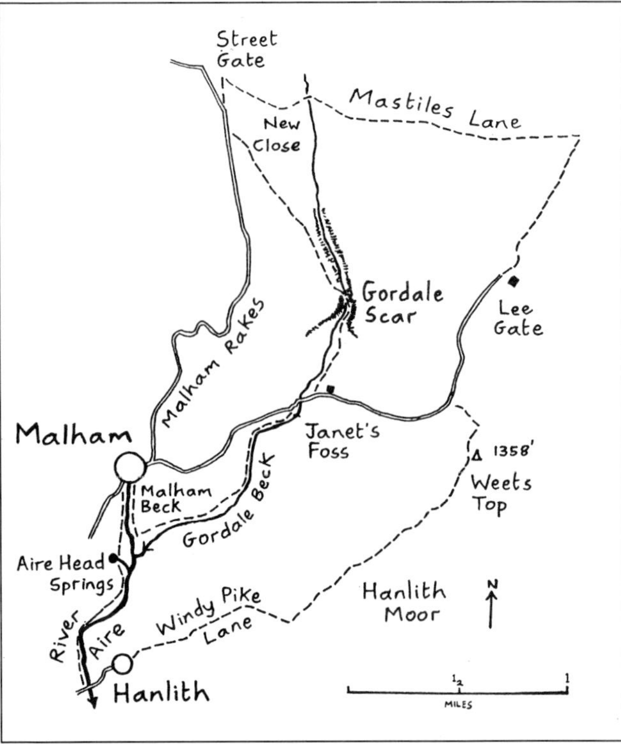

Wayside cross base, Mastiles Lane

Start:
Malham
Distance:
9½ miles
Map:
1:25,000 - Yorkshire Dales South
1:50,000 - Landranger 98

the ravine delayed the moment of impact. Two waterfalls await, one flowing over the worn rocks to be scaled, the other pouring through a window high above. In the turmoil of spate the beck can run amok, challenging anyone to clamber through the gorge. In normal conditions the short climb holds few terrors, despite the holds worn smooth through the passage of countless visitors. It is worth noting that its descent is a less simple proposition, particularly if there is a queue of folk impatiently waiting to come up.

A scamper up a scree-strewn path gave way to the agoraphobic moor-top, where green and white each own half-shares in the landscape. The elongated gorge of the upper valley of Gordale Beck stretches away between terraced scars, but this selfishly guarded natural line can only be taken by the intrepid free-spirit. Showing an unhealthy respect for the rights of the privileged landowner, I chose instead to follow the attractive path across to the Malham Tarn road to join Mastiles Lane at Street Gate, where an old roadsign still announced the miles to Grassington.

In the foot and hoof steps of monks bound to and from Fountains Abbey, drovers with their cattle and traders with packhorses, this historic highway rolled timelessly on towards Kilnsey in Wharfedale. The surviving base of a wayside cross was passed before it became enclosed: while the walls add character, they would have been conspicuous by their absence in monastic times. It was left with regret for exposed Lee Gate Farm, above which the sight of frozen sheep carcasses huddled pathetically under a wall-high December snowdrift reminded me that the hard-pressed hill farmer views a Pennine winter rather differently to the hillwalker.

As the road dropped towards Gordale I kept faith with high ground to reach the walk's summit on Weets Top. Here a multiplicity of parishes send remote arms up to a communal meeting place, where an Ordnance column presides over a comprehensive circle of the Craven uplands. Pointing skyward with greater conviction, however, is the restored Weets Cross which occupies an inferior position tucked away at the top of the lane.

An unusual glimpse down into the ravine of Gordale

Hanlith Moor's rough pastures set the scene for a prolonged downhill strike, becoming enclosed as Windy Pike Lane ushered me into the hamlet of Hanlith. The final leg embraces the Pennine Way again, though a more logical path saw me passing the manorial cornmill on the opposite bank. This carried the bonus of witnessing the 're-birth' of the Aire at the resurgent waters of Aire Head Springs. Here Malham Water - which last saw daylight at Water Sinks, below Malham Tarn - gushes enthusiastically out of an unassuming field, and within yards meets Gordale and Malham Becks to form an instant river.

The approach to the Scar

13: AROUND MALHAM MOOR

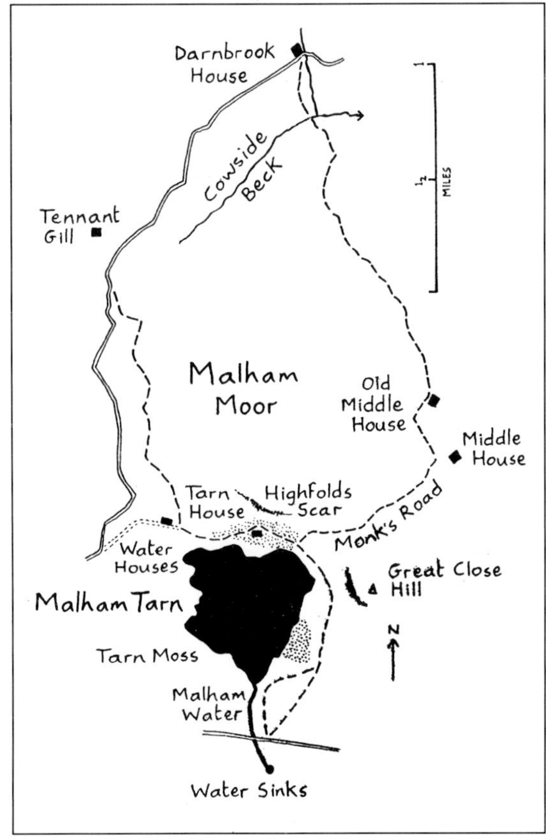

At Malham Tarn

Start: Malham Tarn
Distance: 8 miles
Map: 1:25,000 - Yorkshire Dales South
1:50,000 - Landranger 98

The limestone uplands of Malham Moor are a two tone paradise to which this walk adds the wonders of the tarn. Outflowing Malham Water meets the moor road at Water Sinks Gate, bound for a subterranean passage at nearby Water Sinks. Saving that for the end, stride out across the moor to bring the steely waters of the tarn into view, joining the drive to Malham Tarn House under the watchful eye of gleaming Great Close Scar.

Leaving tarn and house for study on the way back, seek out the grassy saddle below Great Close Hill, key to the hidden farm of Middle House. At restored Old Middle House, Norse farmers paved the way for those from Fountains Abbey, evidence that sheep have for so long been all-important on these hills. It is not easy now to picture the scene two centuries ago when the greatest cattle fairs in the north took place on the extensive pasture of Great Close, beasts being driven hundred of miles from north of the border. A further indication of monastic importance is underfoot, in the delectable green road to Arncliffe known as the Monk's Road. On the brow above Middle House its seductive turf must be left for another day, as the destination now is the farmstead of Darnbrook: though the present house dates largely from the 17th century, the farmstead knew the all-powerful grip of Fountains.

Encroachment into the gathering grounds of the Wharfe by way of Cowside Beck and the Skirfare exacts its toll with a mile and a half of uphill road walking, though verges cushion much of the journey. At the drive to Tennant Gill the Pennine Way is picked up, crossing pleasant pastures to approach the tarn. This time enter the wooded grounds to reach the house itself, a somewhat austere establishment that for many years has been leased from the National Trust as a field studies centre. It originated as a shooting lodge for Lord Ribblesdale in the late 18th century, later much changed into a family home by Walter Morrison.

The return to the moor road gives time to reflect on the tarn and its bleak surroundings. The monks stocked the waters that to this day are probed by the enthusiastic hunter of trout, while the first thing every student is taught on arrival is the explanation for this vast sheet of water in an archetypal limestone landscape: can we all answer in unison ...'impervious Silurian slate, sir!'

above: *Malham Tarn and Highfolds Scar*

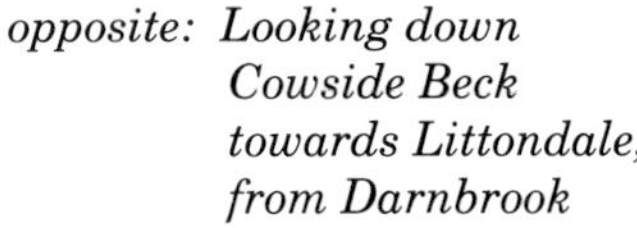

opposite: *Looking down Cowside Beck towards Littondale, from Darnbrook*

right: *Great Close Scar*

CHAPTER THREE THREE PEAKS COUNTRY

WALK 14 SMEARSETT SCAR, FEIZOR & THE RIBBLE 62

WALK 15 THE HEART OF RIBBLESDALE 66

WALK 16 BLEA MOOR & DENT HEAD 68

WALK 17 FLINTER GILL & THE RIVER DEE 72

WALK 18 BARBON BECK & BULLPOT 75

The noble mountains of Whernside, Ingleborough and Penyghent have lent their collective title to the region of valleys divided by rolling fells in the south-western corner of the Dales. The hills here climb to the west of the Pennine watershed, and with the following chapter are the only areas to see their waters flow west to the Irish Sea. Chief rivers are the Ribble and Dee, rising in the same bleak uplands but immediately turning away from each other. The fair Dee forms the northern limits of Three Peaks Country, carving a deep incision as it curves a precise course down towards Sedbergh. With only a narrow road running its length, it has to this day remained one of the Dales' backwaters, and its little capital of Dent retains that same unchanged charisma.

The Ribble, meanwhile, is a Three Peaks river through and through until leaving the higher ground behind at Settle. It divides Ingleborough and Penyghent while showing allegiance to the latter: the extensive triangle of the Ingleborough massif looks out over several valleys, and claims a number of villages around its base. Whernside is another peak of immense girth, dominating Ribblehead and sprawling many miles down into Dentdale. All three of these giants spawn walks on their accommodating flanks.

Two widely publicised elements of the district are the Settle-Carlisle Line and the Three Peaks Walk, each of which has had a torrid time in recent years. Saved from closure by the skin of its teeth, the railway runs the length of Ribblesdale in its climb from Settle, and traverses the head of Dentdale so that in most corners of Three Peaks Country it might be evident. The fabled big walk, meanwhile, has inflicted extensive damage on the peaks, though the solitary walker can still devise a rewarding walk over each of them, independent of the other two.

Happily, less delicate terrain decorates the mountains' lower slopes, with the shapely profiles of the high tops serving as overpowering backdrops. Here the waters drain underground at every opportunity, resulting in the remarkable features that only limestone country can produce. A wealth of green roads link a profusion of scars, pavements and caves, interspersed with awesome potholes and spectacular waterfalls: quite literally, we only touch the surface.

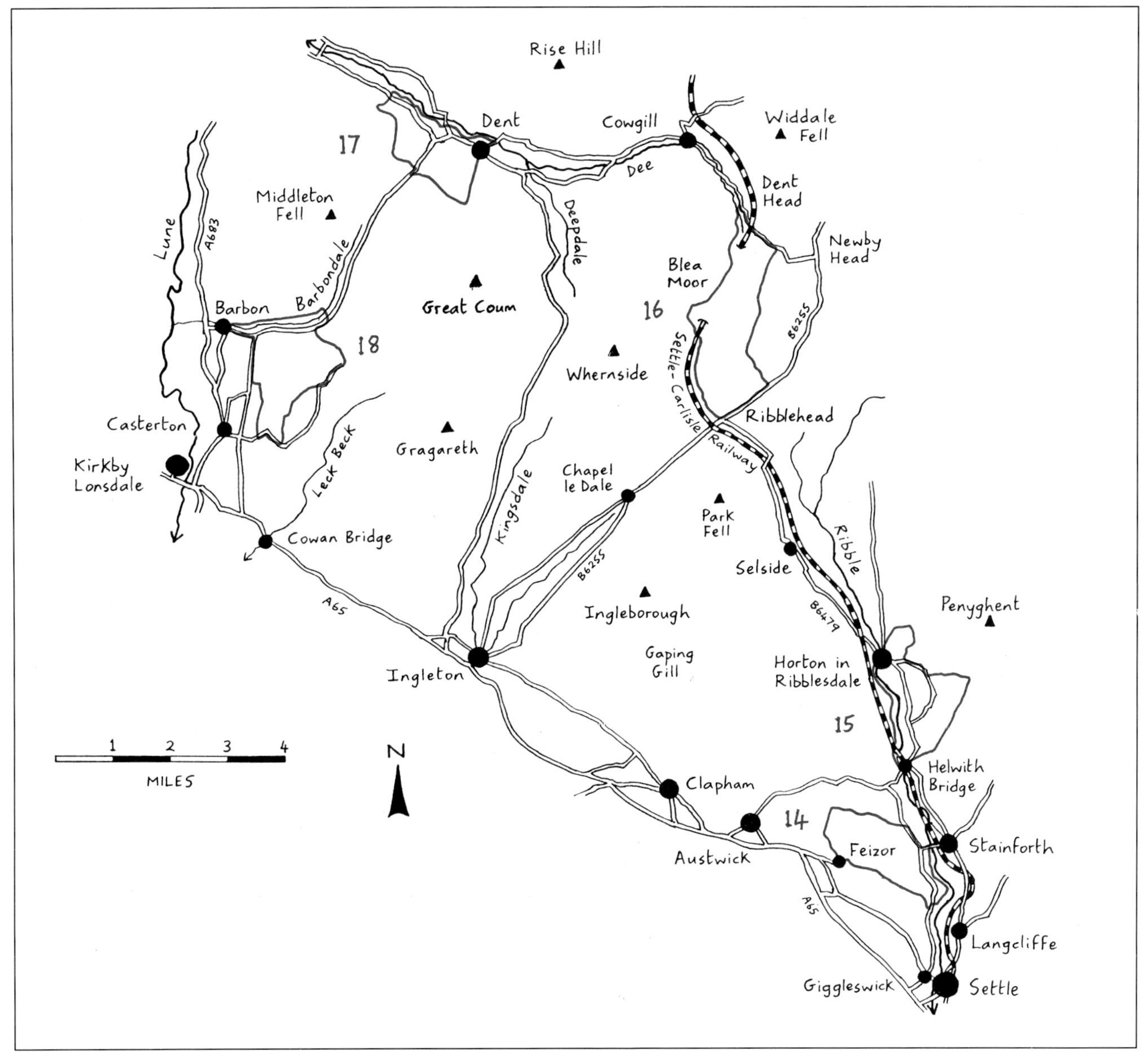

14: SMEARSETT SCAR, FEIZOR AND THE RIBBLE

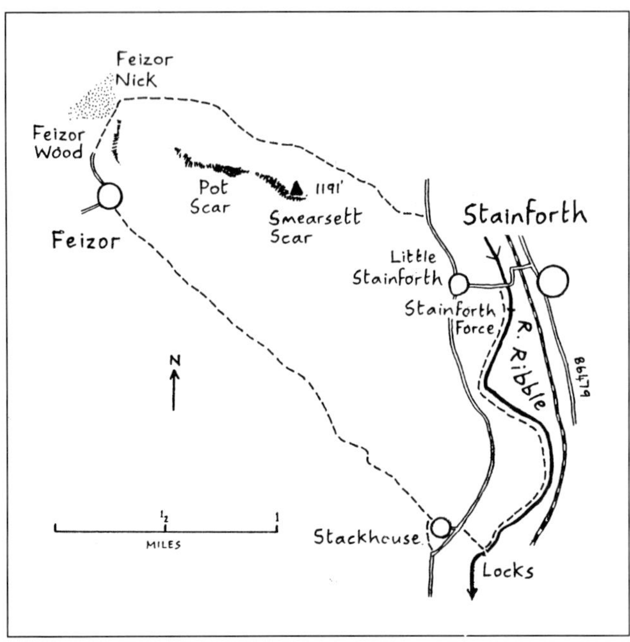

above: *The summit, Smearsett Scar*
below: *Walkers by the Ribble admire Stainforth Bridge (note the cat)*
opposite: *Penyghent, pride of Ribblesdale, from above Stackhouse*

Start:
Stainforth
Distance:
7½ miles
Map:
1:25,000 - Yorkshire Dales West
1:50,000 - Landranger 98

Settle, Horton and Clapham enclose a gleaming triangle of limestone country, a treasure house of delights bedecked with pavements, scars and crags. This circuit in the southern half of the area carries a riverside finale for dessert.

From Stainforth cross both road and railway to the 17th century packhorse bridge looping elegantly over the Ribble. The sparkling waterfall downstream combines to make this a popular spot for visitors, and is perhaps best saved for the finish, on a natural up-river approach. Knight Stainforth Hall presides over the shrunken hamlet of Little Stainforth, and this square-set 17th century giant sees you off to the hills. The path to the defile of Feizor Nick is best noted for its view updale to Penyghent, for the main feature in the immediate vicinity is out of sight and passed without notice. Smearsett Scar is a striking limestone upthrust, turning its back on the path yet only a minute away up a grassy pasture. Its crest is a favourite place of repose, and a peerless vantage point for our triangle.

The path runs on to the rough road through Feizor Nick, utilising it to drop down into one of the Dales' lesser lights, the hamlet of Feizor. It is a motorists' cul de sac, and who would wish it otherwise? An attractive grouping of cottages is enhanced by Smearsett's colleague Pot Scar brooding over: Feizor's farming life is also as dominant however, in the presence of droppings so prevalent in such environs. Farm droppings are not the throughput of its livestock, but the characteristic leftovers of redundant machinery, fencing, feedbags, rubble and general clutter that confirm this as a working environment and not a chocolate-box scene.

Return to the Ribble is by way of an ambling path through the hills, falling more sharply at the other end to find a way round the jealously guarded privacy of Stackhouse. At Locks the river is finally regained, and the way upstream clings tightly to waters that are generally far less accessible than most Dales' rivers. Making the most of this opportunity, the path nevertheless is quick to arrive back at the falls, now better appreciated in their well favoured setting.

Neighbouring Pot Scar and the distant Bowland Moors from the crest of Smearsett

Cottages at Feizor

Stainforth Force

15: THE HEART OF RIBBLESDALE

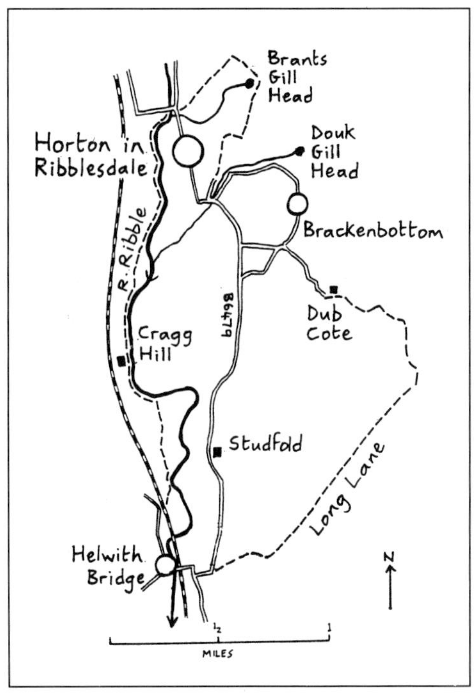

Penyghent from Horton, November morning

Horton is the nerve-centre of Three Peaks country, but on this occasion I chose merely to tread the flanks of Penyghent and enjoy spacious views across to its taller colleagues rather than scale any of them. The opening move was a rare Ribbleside stroll: below Horton it flows unadventurously through fields, the ever-present spectre of limestone quarries eclipsed by Penyghent's noble profile. It would be superfluous to impart the information that this section has been adopted as part of the Ribble Way, for the little logo leaping out at every twist in the path forced a conclusion that long-distance walkers are assumed to be incapable of using map or guide. Concentration of meagre resources into such projects can only deflect funds from more pressing if less prestigious footpath issues.

Little more than an inn, a combined rail/river bridge and a corner for quarry waggons to take on two wheels, Helwith Bridge was my ticket to the hills. A long, long trail - what else but Long Lane - carried me at a well-judged slant across the underbelly of the crouching lion. Like many of its ilk its stony start soon blossomed into a smashing green road, height being gained painlessly. The devastation of Ribblesdale's quarries receded with every step as the hoary giant of Ingleborough shrugged off this insolent snapping at its ankles. More distantly Whernside chipped in its less glamorous contribution, and with Penyghent but a stone's throw ahead, I felt as one with the Three Peaks without labouring round their tortured paths.

My green highway finally shrugged off its walls, and all too soon a return to the valley was being contemplated: certainly there were no obstacles to remaining on this fine track for a more ambitious finish over Penyghent's summit, but rain clouds were gathering, and the day would have been overshadowed by reflections on an ascent in perfect conditions only weeks earlier. So instead it was rapidly down the pastures to Dub Cote bunkbarn, where a sign declared that boots should not be taken inside: I could only generously assume that there was some form of ante-room they could be left, or was the place only geared up for the motorist?

The farming hamlet of Brackenbottom nestles on a narrow lane, and though I was on the fringe of Horton, a worthwhile variation finish took me along a network of rough lanes to the spectacle of Brants Gill Head, where the stream that sank at Hunt Pot, several hundred feet higher, returns to daylight with abounding enthusiasm. Horton was still waiting patiently below, and the welcome return to the Horton social scene of the Golden Lion after a dry 18 years ensured a similar welcome for me.

above: *The Ribble at Horton*

below: *Cheek by jowl at Horton - St. Oswald's Church and the Golden Lion*

Start:
Horton in Ribblesdale
Distance:
$6^{1/2}$ miles
Map:
1:25,000 - Yorkshire Dales West
1:50,000 - Landranger 98

16: BLEA MOOR AND DENT HEAD

above:
A northbound train prepares to cross Ribblehead Viaduct

top right:
Delicate harebells on Ribblehead's limestone pastures

right:
Whernside's summit ridge from Blea Moor's isolated signal box

Just off the beaten track - Force Gill

Start:
Ribblehead
Distance:
9 miles
Map:
1:25,000 - Yorkshire Dales West
1:50,000 - Landranger 98

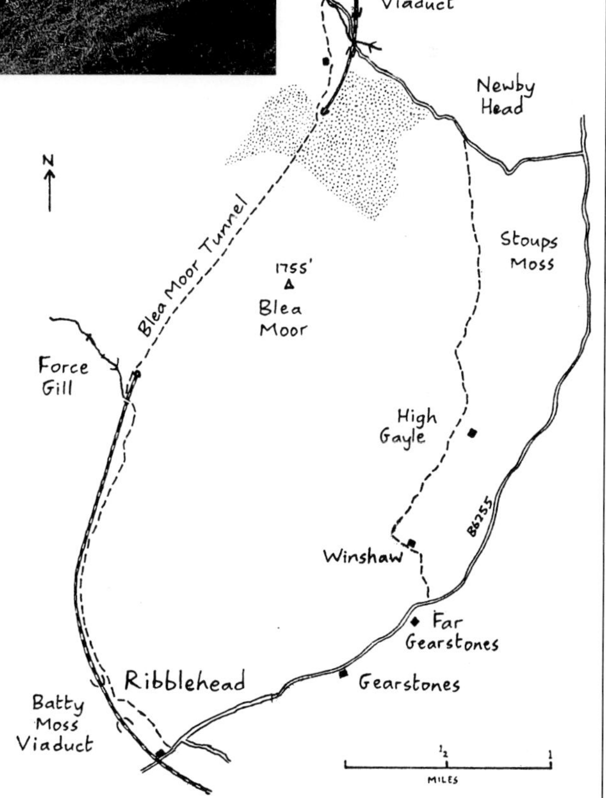

Railway country + mountain country = viaducts, and so it is that the looping arches of the Settle-Carlisle line are pre-eminent features of this bracing tramp. The upper reaches of both Dentdale and Ribblesdale achieve an awesome bleakness which only serves to heighten the sense of grandeur of this fabled and much-loved railway. Batty Moss Viaduct (popularly Ribblehead) is, as symbol of the line that in 1989 was saved from closure only by the efforts of a well organised pressure group, a fitting place to start the walk.

Without passing beneath any of the majestic 24 arches, a path picks its way along the lineside route that has changed out of all recognition since 'Three Peakers' were sent to churn it up as penance for creating the scarred direct route up Whernside. Beyond the supreme isolation of Blea Moor signal box the line is crossed on an aqueduct prior to the longest of its tunnels, which burrows 350 feet below the moor. No such clandestine prospects for the path, which chooses the open air version along a row of air shafts pinpointing the line's presence far below.

Where the line plunges into darkness, this interesting corner of Whernside's sprawling flanks reveals Force Gill making some impressive splashes and sees an old pack-route, the Craven Way, continue its own crossing to Dentdale. On descending from Blea Moor to the black hole which releases the trains, the panorama reaches far beyond Dentdale's verdant floor to the Howgill Fells and, on a clear day, the arresting heights of Lakeland. Involvement with Dentdale's greenery is limited to a few pastures below Dent Head Viaduct, gained after a steep haul up the winding road from the cosy nook of Bridge End. Dent Head vies with nearby twin Arten Gill as the most dramatic viaduct on the line, for both span deep-cut gills. Under the arches will be found a lovely picnic spot by a dwarfed pack-bridge.

Back on the heights a last look back over the viaduct can be taken before striking out again over open country. Yorkshire's famous triumvirate of mountains return to enhance a cold landscape, and in time the road at Far Gearstones is met. This old Lancaster-Richmond turnpike leads unerringly to Ribblehead, with options to venture off to discover either hidden caves on the right, or the equally hidden charms of Thorns Gill down to the left.

above: *Ingleborough and Ribblehead Viaduct from Gearstones*

opposite: *The majestic Dent Head Viaduct*

right: *An attractive corner at Bridge End, Dent Head. The path crosses this delightful bridge*

17: FLINTER GILL AND THE RIVER DEE

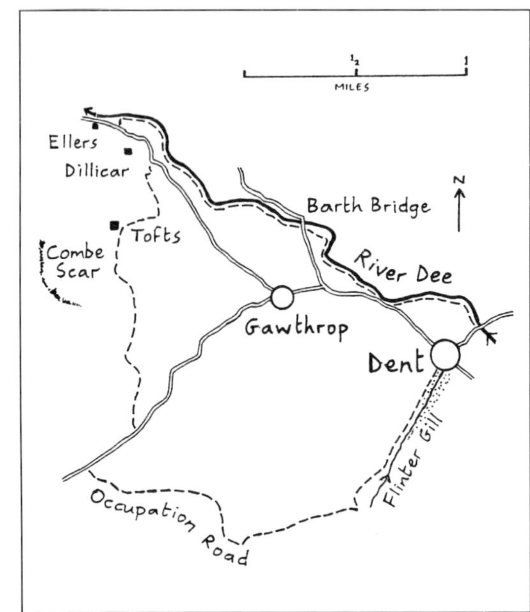

opposite top:
At the head of Flinter Gill, with lower Dentdale framed by Combe Scar and the Howgill Fells

opposite bottom:
On the lush banks of the Dee

right:
The steep wall of Calf Top from the end of the Occupation Road at Barbon Head

below:
The rugged wall of Combe Scar from Barth Bridge

The little town of Dent - for a town is what it was, at least - is a place set apart from other Dales communities: there's only one Dent, and on entering its confines, one can readily appreciate its uniqueness. This grand exercise merges fellside and riverbank, and in doing so combines extensive vistas over Dentdale with the intimacy of the Dee's green banks.

Flinter Gill drains the northern flanks of Great Coum in the manner of all such mountain streams, but in its lower reaches it sets a higher standard to tumble - should its waters not already have gone to ground - through a ravine bedecked in exquisite foliage, bound as straight as an arrow for the homely cluster of whitewashed cottages at its foot.

It can be traced by way of its parallel outrake, firstly beneath oaks that hide the sun, then up a constantly improving trackway to emerge onto the Occupation Road. Immediate delights are replaced by distant scenes as purposeful strides lap up this green lane. While it becomes progressively stonier underfoot, this detracts little from the upland panorama: the unbroken face of Middleton Fell, directly ahead, is a foil to the more distant, rounded tops of the Howgill Fells blocking the foot of Dentdale.

In due course the pass between Barbon and Dent is gained, and within minutes a super path is Dentdale bound, dropping down below the monumental scoop of Combe Scar. An absence of obvious routes thereto leave it as something to gaze upon rather than walk upon. Nevertheless it is a strikingly colourful addition to the Dentdale scene, exhibiting a cragginess otherwise unknown in the dale. From the forlorn ruins of Combe House a path spirals to the valley floor, where a back road shadows the Dee. Almost at once the riverbank is claimed by a path slavishly clinging to the unsullied river, never more than the odd stride from its singing waters. Through the final pastures the huddle of Dent's cottages around its mother church perch above, with the Megger Stones marking a striking Dent skyline much higher. As the cobbled streets finally echo the clatter of boots, they can turn in for a well earned pint, and not just any old glassful but one caringly brewed in this very dale!

Barth Bridge

Start:
Dent
Distance:
$6^{1}/_{2}$ miles
Map:
1:25,000 - Yorkshire Dales West
1:50,000 - Landranger 98

18: AROUND CASTERTON FELL

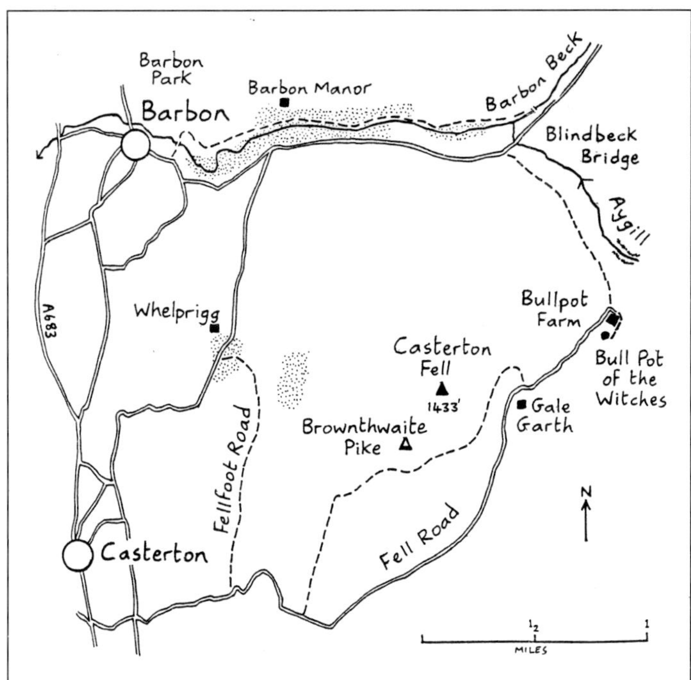

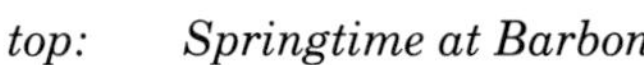
top: *Springtime at Barbon*

below: *The flanks of Castle Knott fall to Barbon Beck*

Start:	*Barbon*
Distance:	*8½ miles*
Map:	*1:25,000 - Pathfinder 628 (SD67/68)*
	1:50,000 - Landranger 97 & 98 (just)

Nowhere is the errant nature of the National Park boundary better condemned than in the west of the district, where the Middleton, Barbon and Leck Fells are omitted because they happened to be in Westmorland or Lancashire at the time. This walk explores the heart of the area, where Casterton Fell sits between its more mountainous neighbours and fellow outcasts.

The village of Barbon hides off the beaten track, at the start of a minor road through the hills from the Lune valley to Dent. Its church sees a drive off into the parkland of Barbon Manor, to be quickly eschewed in order to pursue a broad track along the thickly wooded bank of Barbon Beck. Beyond the trees the vibrant waters lead up to a simple footbridge, though a ford just before it offers a minor short-cut if the water is low.

This quiet corner is a pleasant picnic spot for the discerning few who know it, but as it's far too early in this walk locate the beginnings of a track up the open fell downstream. This is the northern flank of Casterton Fell, mounted effortlessly to the terminus of a green lane leading to Bullpot Farm: towards the top a glimpse of rougher ground should be sufficient to detour to the ravine of Aygill, where rowan fill the rock-walled incisions in otherwise grassy surrounds.

At Bullpot, what might be termed a cavers' road grinds to a halt, and the environs of the old farmhouse will again delay the inquisitive. This is cavers' Mecca, being an important club base in deference to the area's underground qualities. Famous holes abound, and just below the farm such gloomy recesses as Lancaster Hole, County Pot and the caverns of Ease Gill lurk. Most handily placed is Bull Pot of the Witches, only a couple of minutes from the house. As long as there's some water about, then a long fall teems into the darkness, but such are its defences that it can only be witnessed with the utmost caution.

From its terminus in the hills the fell road winds down to Casterton, and not only is it abandoned well before then, but a branch part-way along takes in a higher crossing of Casterton Fell. Its summit is served by an Ordnance column, while its second top of note is proudly occupied by a walloping cairn on a great rash of stones: this is Brownthwaite Pike, a superb vantage point for the Lune valley, and only a short pull from the fine track underfoot. A Romanesque green lane drops back onto the fell road, again soon vacated for Fellfoot Lane. This enclosed way forges a long mile's passage, constantly improving and living up to its name: at its demise, an unfenced back road takes over, maintaining the promenade along the base of the fell that has been the central feature.

In Barbon Village

Brownthwaite Pike, looking to Gragareth

Middleton Fell and Crag Hill from the summit of Casterton Fell

On the Fellfoot Road under Casterton Fell

CHAPTER FOUR THE HOWGILL FELLS

WALK 19	CAUTLEY SPOUT & THE RAWTHEY	80
WALK 20	CROOK, WINDER & ARANT HAW	85
WALK 21	CARLIN GILL & BLACK FORCE	89
WALK 22	BORROWDALE & THE LUNE GORGE	93
WALK 23	THE ASCENT OF GREEN BELL	96

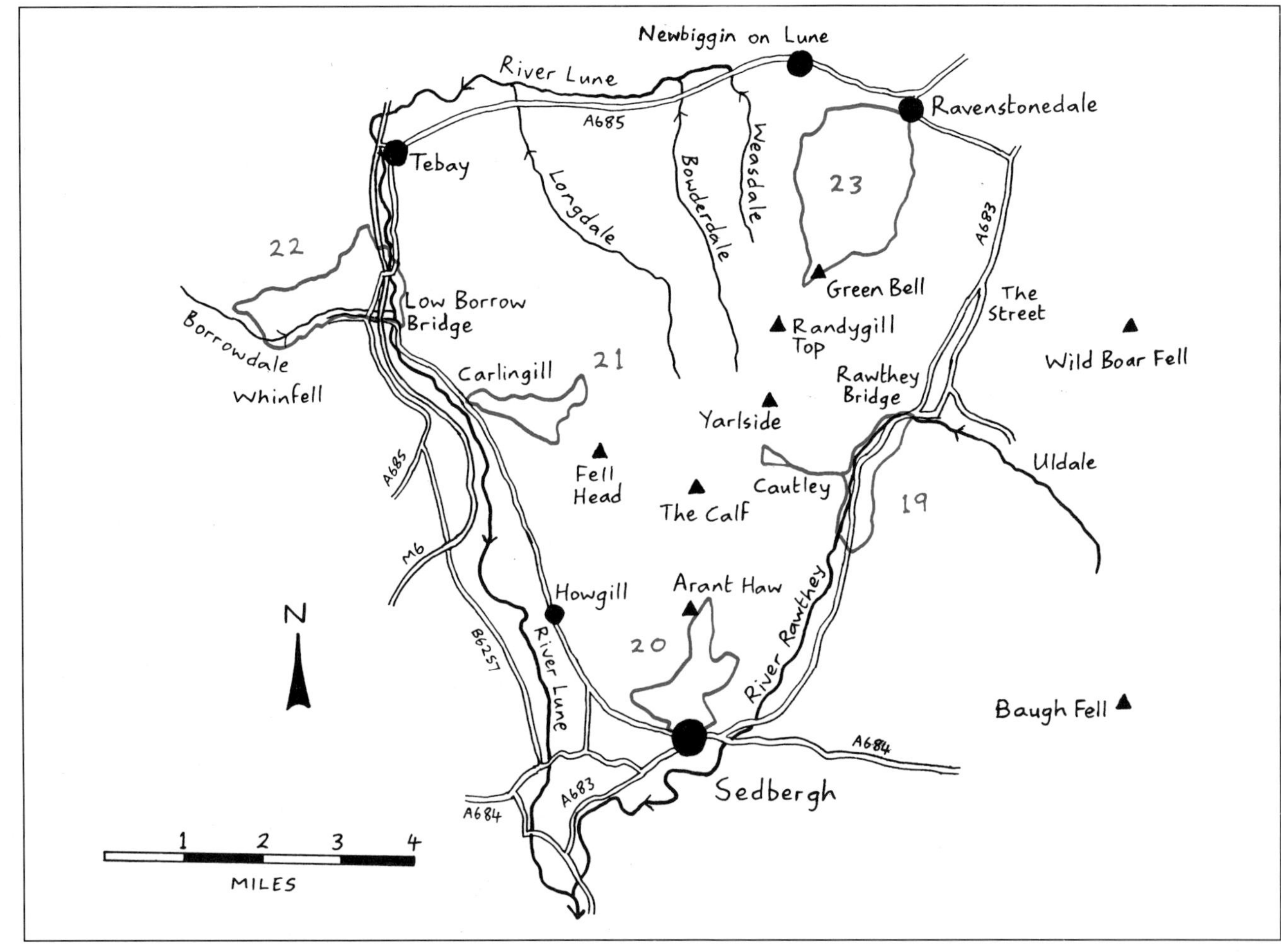

Concisely defined by the river Lune to north and west and the river Rawthey to the east, the triangular mass of the Howgill Fells is a walkers' paradise. At the sharp end sits Sedbergh, a pre-eminent base for the walker, while the villages of Tebay and Ravenstonedale occupy the other two corners. Outside of this zone, similar country is happy to be associated with the Howgills, in the shape of lovely Borrowdale and its ridges to the west, and Garsdale and the headwaters of the Rawthey to the east. The name of these hills is derived from a tiny hamlet along the western base, and until recent times even this was not reflected on Ordnance maps.

Castle Fell and Mabbin Crag from the banks of Borrow Beck

Only the section of the Howgills that was part of the old West Riding is given National Park status, and it does seem bizarre that one stride across a gill or a tussock of grass will take you into mountain country that is accorded no recognition at all. The terrain is conducive to wide strides and views to match, with steep flanks and long ridge-tops packed tightly into a compact upland tract: nothing is wasted here. Probably the greatest of the Howgills' assets is the fact that above the intake walls, the hills are free of obstruction, and a long-standing freedom to roam sets them well apart from some of the hill country in the Dales. The slaty nature of the underlying rock erupts to prominence at Cautley and Carlin Gill to further betray its true allegiance to the Lakeland lifestyle.

19: CAUTLEY SPOUT AND THE RAWTHEY

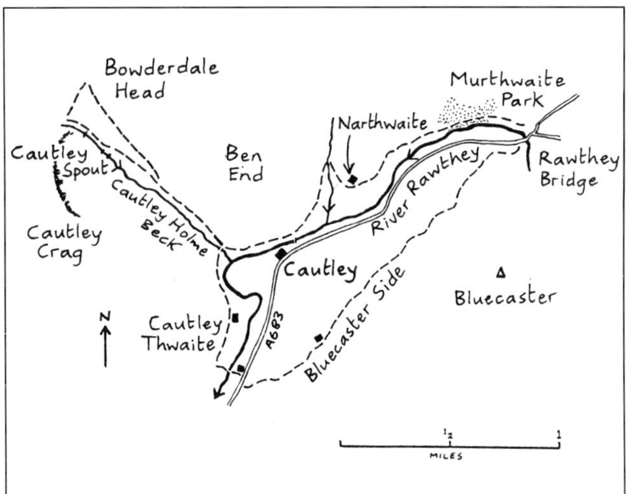

The Cross Keys Inn at Cautley boasts a location so enviable that its temperance tendencies can be overlooked - the scenery is sufficiently intoxicating. All-powerful Cautley Crag leans on the cascades of Cautley Spout, and such is its magnetism that the walk's opening steps will draw incredulous looks from others embarking on the said pilgrimage: on this occasion, intimate study of the Spout is to be saved until the end of the walk, which turns for now up Rawthey's bank. The route assumes a variety of guises by way of Backside Beck, the austere farm settlement of Narthwaite and the serenity of Murthwaite Park.

Rawthey Bridge straddles the river's major turning point, as it turns to demarcate the eastern boundary of the Howgill Fells. Forsaking its banks, head south to climb a sunken course to a magnificent terrace on the grassy flanks of Bluecaster Side. This classic route is the old road to Kirkby Stephen, a green conveyer-belt from which to enjoy the massed ranks

Cautley Crag and Spout from the Cross Keys, with the slopes behind rising to the Calf

Yarlside's south top escapes the wreathes of mist, as seen from above the upper falls

opposite, right:
Wild Boar Fell from Narthwaite
opposite, bottom left:
The Rawthey at Cautley
opposite bottom right:
Lower Falls, winter

Yarlside from the old road on Bluecaster Side

Start:
Cautley
Distance:
$6^{1/4}$ miles
Map:
1:25,000 -
Pathfinder 617
(SD69/79)
1:50,000 -
Landranger 98

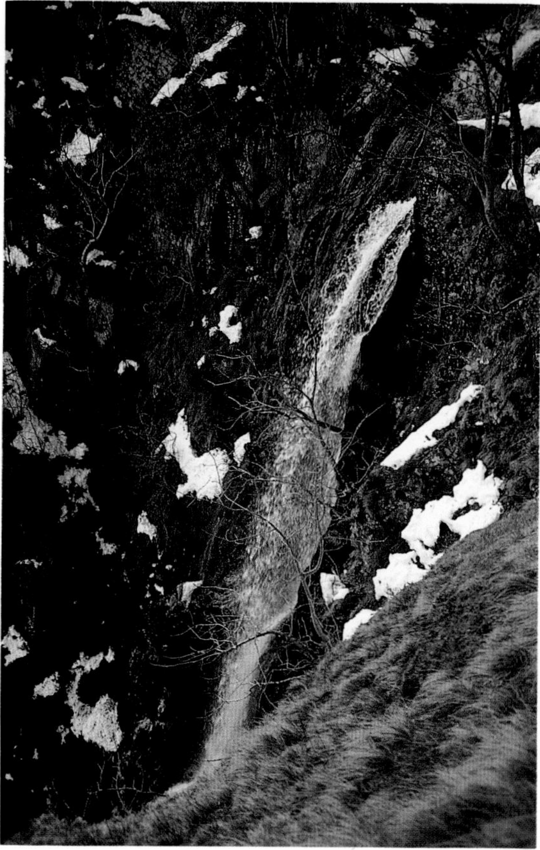

Upper Falls, summer

Looking back to Great Dummacks from Murthwaite Park

of the Howgills, paraded as if only for our benefit. 2000-footers Yarlside and Great Dummacks solidly frame the centrepiece, Cautley's gouged side-valley driving deep into the hills. If all walking was like this we could keep going till nightfall, but beyond Bluecaster Cottage the way falls to the road.

Bridging the Rawthey again, thoughts can turn to the showdown with Cautley Spout. The farmstead at Cautley Thwaite possesses a timeless quality matched by the ageless appeal of gathering conkers (otherwise horse chestnuts) at the edge of its yard - although I was only collecting the best of the windfall for the girls back home, of course. A simple footbridge over Cautley Holme Beck is the true springboard for the Spout, as the tourist path is joined to approach its foot.

A grand triangle begins on the path spiralling up by the edge of the ravine to allow cautious glimpses into its recesses. Above the partially camouflaged main waterfall, a more accessible series of falls can be lingered over. From here a useful trod cuts along to the grassy saddle of Bowderdale Head, the pass between the Howgills' two highest mountains, Yarlside and The Calf. Ensuring not to go through this green defile and so involve an umpteen-mile return, another splendid path soon forms to slant down Yarlside's flank to return to the footbridge at Cautley, and the cup that cheers.

20: CROOK, WINDER AND ARANT HAW

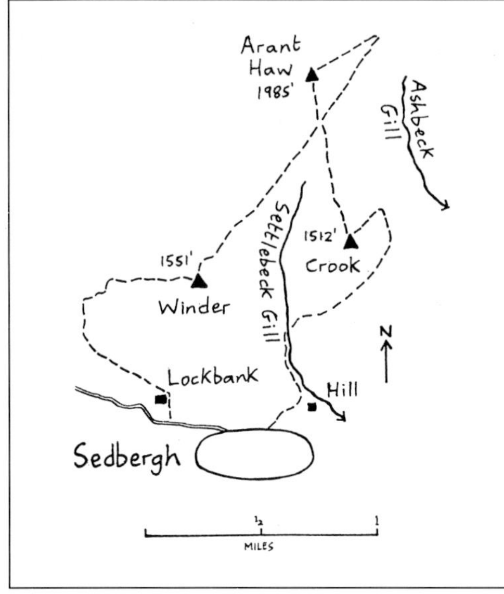

Start:	*Sedbergh*
Distance:	*5½ miles*
Map:	*1:25,000 - Pathfinder 617 (SD69/79) 1:50,000 - Landranger 97 & 98*

The tempting path continuing to Calders from the shoulder of Arant Haw

'Sedbergh and the Howgills' - just the mention is enough to have me reaching for the boots. This cornerstone of the Dales never fails to deliver the goods, and this walk links up the three typically rounded tops nearest the Howgill capital.

The royal road out of town is ushered on its way by a battery of discreet signs, to climb by Settlebeck Gill to the untethered spaces of 'the fell'. If Winder didn't already tower over Sedbergh, it's certainly towering now. On crossing the beck below Winder's gaunt wall, a lovely waterfall delays the start up a raking path encompassing Crook's bracken-clad girth. The pull to its crest finds a surprisingly fine cairn - and a general character not usually associated with Howgill summits - and more importantly reveals both its more coveted twin Winder, and their guardian, Arant Haw.

Slanting across to regain the trade-route through the Howgills at the head of Settlebeck Gill, Arant Haw's uppermost flanks are out-manoeuvred by the path, and taking full advantage, rise stealthily to the shoulder of the fell. Before doubling back, a break is demanded to appraise the revered cluster that is the inner sanctum of Howgill-land.

The broad path motors invitingly on through a saddle to climb to Calders, and it will take much willpower to forego this undemanding continuation to both it and thence The Calf itself. If time, conditions,

above:
Settlebeck Gill

above right:
The summit of Crook

right:
Fell Head and the western ridges of the Calf group from Arant Haw

above left:
The summit of Arant Haw, with the Calf, Bram Rigg Top and Calders ranged beyond

above:
Arant Haw from the west ridge of Fell Head

Arant Haw and Winder from across the Lune

and fitness are in accord, then off you go, and we'll see you back on the prow of Arant Haw, a meagre 15 feet short of the 2000ft line.

With Crook and Winder crouching obediently below, the route to the latter is a matter of little conjecture, as green ways lead first down to the trusty trade-route and then mount tame flanks to Winder's cairn and trig. point. In the light of an Autumn evening one can contemplate the awesome wonder of it all (or merely what time the pubs open) in the knowledge that a scurry down the front would have Howgill Lane underfoot in a quarter-hour. When it is time to be dragged away, however, the finest option takes up the offer of a green carpet heading away from the sleepy little town. It runs westward down to the intake wall, there deflected by it to slant down to Lockbank Farm, where 'the fell' will, more so than most, be departed with regret.

21: CARLIN GILL AND BLACK FORCE

Carlingill Beck and Uldale Head

Blease Fell and a more distant Borrowdale from the path above Black Force

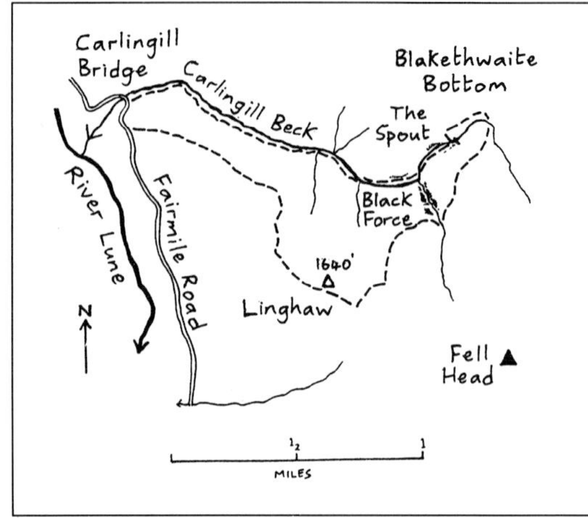

Start: *Carlingill Bridge*
GR: 624996
Distance: *4½ miles*
Map: *1:25,000 - Pathfinder 617 (SD69/79)*
1:50,000 - Landranger 97

The adage that a lot goes into a little should be borne in mind when allotting time to this apparently modest trek, for it embraces sections that shouldn't, indeed can't, be hurried. Anyone unaware of the hidden wonders of Carlin Gill will be in line for the most memorable of surprises as he sallies forth along the path shadowing Carlingill Beck, probing deeply into the folds of the hills but as yet unaware of what lies in store: all around is grassy and serene, while up on the skyline a group of ponies graze the breezier heights. It is hard now to imagine that virtually all of this walk is within the old West Riding, sharing common ground with Sheffield but not Tebay!

At inflowing Small Gill a chirpy waterfall tenders a pleasant aside as the valley narrows to the width of the beck in its low gorge. When progress looks debatable, crossing the stream sheds light on a stamped out trod traversing the harsh scree slopes. All too soon the moment is gone, but there is no time for regrets as you are deposited with impeccable precision at the very foot of Black Force. The location of this ravine has been in no doubt for some time, but now you are placed firmly at its base, its soaring lines fully warrant a silent tribute.

At the confluence a decision must be made. The most direct continuation involves getting to grips with the rib shielding the Black Force ravine, a tantalising prospect. The longer alternative finds further adventure on the floor of Carlin Gill, tracing another well stamped path between broken walls worthy of a Lakeland gill. Beyond a delicious waterslide the highlight of this escapade tentatively reveals itself, as the fittingly named Spout spills into an amphitheatre that bars further progress. Be sure to get as close as possible, as walkers have been known to make their escape with the Spout still hidden behind a projecting rib.

opposite: The Spout

The finest exit faces up to an angled slate wall on the left, a natural scramble above which a sheeptrod runs along to the secret basin of Blakethwaite Bottom, amid the deafening silence of a Howgills sanctuary. A path on the opposite bank traverses back along to the head of Black Force, all the while procuring an inspiring study of Carlin Gill far below. A similar path takes up the reins around this northern butt of Fell Head, clinging doggedly to its contour to work a way round to a saddle linking Linghaw with its parent fell. Here a slim trod surmounts the grassy pudding to decline in prolonged manner to the open road above Carlingill Bridge.

Early in the descent the Spout, so shy earlier, makes yet another farewell appearance, while out from the Howgills is a wide panorama across the Lune Gorge to the knobbly tops above Borrowdale and the more distant Lakeland heights. I worked hard at delaying this conclusion in order to squeeze every drop of pleasure out of this final stage, for the waters of Morecambe Bay had taken on a golden veneer, and the pink Lakeland horizon brought Mickledore and the dome of Gable almost within reach.

left: *Black Force*
below: *Evening light over the Lune, seen from Linghaw*

22: BORROWDALE AND THE LUNE GORGE

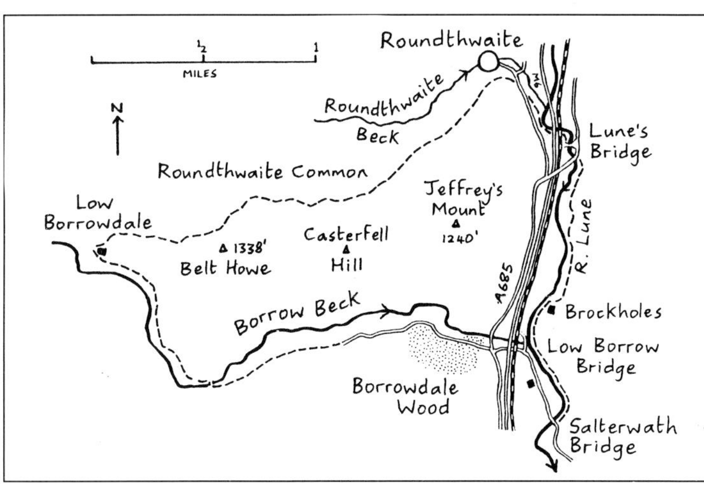

Borrow Beck and Mabbin Crag

Start:	*Low Borrow Bridge*
	GR: 609014
Distance:	*7¼ miles*
Map:	*1:25,000 - English Lakes SE Sheet & Pathfinder 607 (NY60/70)*
	1:50,000 - Landranger 91

Undeniably Lakeland in character, Borrowdale slips quietly out of the Lake District to enjoy its finest miles in the no-man's-land twixt Lakes and Dales. Indeed, the walk's mid-point is nearer the Lake District boundary, though few of its millions of fans will be aware of the place. High and Low Borrow Bridges neatly delineate its bounds, and at either end only farm roads penetrate from the busy main roads threading the hills.

Only Low Borrowdale operates now, one farm in the heart of an unknown hill country. My approach was the obvious one, tracing its access road from the noisy Lune Gorge at Low Borrow Bridge. Though initially surfaced, no cars impinge, and the road cleverly gains just enough height through Borrowdale Woods to emerge with instant views to Whinfell Beacon and its entourage ranged along the south side of the valley. A spell with the crystal beck brought me to this idyllically placed farmstead.

Though tempted to press on updale, I chose on this occasion an exit from the valley by way of a pack-route to Tebay. The simple climb is enriched by views back over the dale before the broad ridge-top wipes the slate clean, and ahead the rangy North Pennines fill the horizon beyond the emasculated railway junction of Tebay and the Westmorland plateau around Orton. A sweeping descent of Roundthwaite Common allows time to pore over a vista which includes the northern ridges of the Howgill Fells. If

the day be good, there are no obstacles to taking advantage of height gained and enjoying a grassy ridgewalk over Belt Howe and Casterfell Hill en route to Jeffrey's Mount out at the end. Its northern shoulder falls lazily to Roundthwaite, though on a fine Sunday morning I had to tread with care as the local lads practised their clay-pigeon shooting on the slopes above the farming hamlet.

Back with the Lune it was time to play musical chairs with the various modes of communication taking full advantage of the most exploitable gap between Richmond and the Cumbrian coast. Roundthwaite Beck's final yards lead to the Lune, about to be belittled by motorway, railway and road high above. The first two cross in tandem, and I sneaked below them on an anglers' path to Lune's Bridge, a beautiful structure that would seem to date from pre-history, seen alongside the modern offerings. Its grey arch strides a foaming gorge, and a bonus of

opposite top:
The Lune funnels through the gorge under Lune's Bridge

opposite bottom:
Primroses on the banks of the Lune

right:
Walkers on the flanks of Jeffrey's Mount survey the Lune Gorge

bottom:
On Roundthwaite Common, looking beyond Orton Scar to the distant North Pennines

being becalmed is that it can be enjoyed in peace. Yards downstream the new Kendal-Tebay road is carried by a mammoth concrete bridge taking river, railway and motorway in one fell swoop. Escaping down the farm road to Brockholes, more natural pictures of the Lune outshout the raucous drone of the M6, and beyond the farm I was at last treated to a worthwhile ramble by Lune's bank, concluding in woodland at Salterwath Bridge.

Up the lane at Low Borrow Bridge the centuries are spanned, from the distinctive outline of a Roman fort through to ultra-modern times. The bridge itself is still in situ, if, like Lune's Bridge, a little overwhelmed by the usurpers. The M6 didn't just steal some of its trade, it took it all, as complete re-alignment of the old road left it similarly high and dry. This at least has saved these graceful bridges from 'improvement', to enjoy their retirement as just another bit of scenery.

23: THE ASCENT OF GREEN BELL

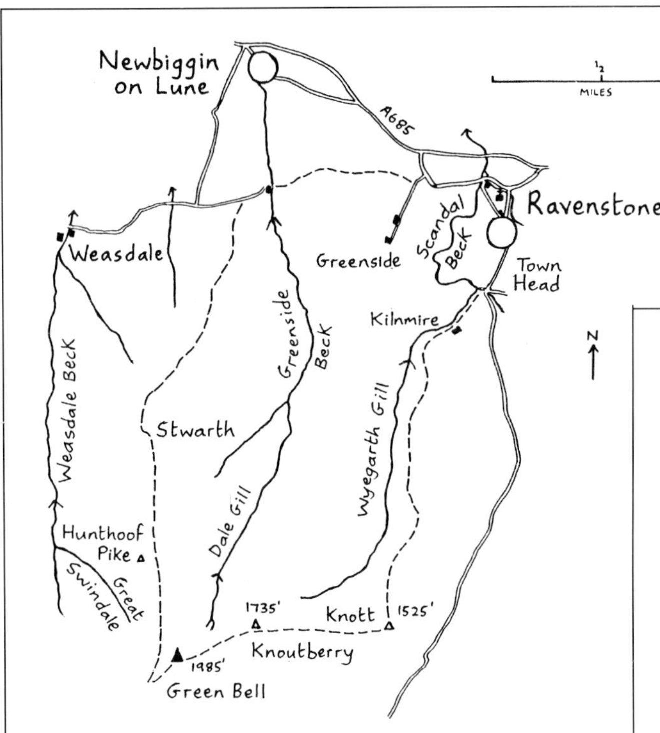

Start:
Ravenstonedale
Distance:
6¾ miles
Map:
1:25,000 - Pathfinder 607 (NY60/70)
1:50,000 - Landranger 91

Fells that narrowly fail to find the 2000ft contour are in general less frequented, yet carry all the advantages of the more popular hills that manage another 50 or 100 feet but cannot improve as viewpoints. The simply yet succinctly named Green Bell is perhaps the finest example, for not only is it marginally short of 'mountain' status, but as a viewpoint it puts many far loftier summits to shame.

Peaceful Ravenstonedale could not provide a more delectable starting point, particularly as its leafy centre is a haven from the heavy waggons bound to or from the motorway at Tebay. Though the Howgill foothills fall to the very bounds of the village, the walk begins with a bridleway - partially an untouched green lane - that sneaks across fields to gain the base of Green Bell's northern shoulder. Open country soon becomes the order of the day, and the inevitable tractor track that characterises these northern Howgill ridges leads off up undemanding gradients. Green Bell could well be scaled without recourse to halts, though Cross Fell and its satellites and an unfolding Lakeland skyline demand such respect. From the rare surface stone on Hunthoof Pike, Green Bell's Ordnance column reveals itself, though a direct pull is better rejected in favour of savouring the ever improving green way of Scot Rake as it slants across to a saddle south-west of the summit.

Looking back to Green Bell from Knott

This moment alone is worth the walk, for its revelation of Green Bell's Howgill Fell colleagues is a real show-stopper. On progressing to the trig. point and scanning the skyline it becomes increasingly difficult to conceive of another summit displaying such a mountain panorama: in fact, for a balanced picture of the bulk of England's mountains, is this modest eminence the supreme observatory? Northwards is the long march of North Pennines from Cross Fell through to Mickle Fell, true summit of Yorkshire; eastwards are the hills of Mallerstang, leading the eye to Ingleborough and the central Dales peaks; next the remarkable Howgills, seen as a well defined mountain group from Green Bell's position of relative detachment; and then across to Lakeland, with the hoary Coniston Fells and Blencathra's unique saddle-roof acting as bookends to a who's who of famous names.

Descent is the simplest of affairs, with the roofs of Ravenstonedale at once in view. After a steep drop to a sheepfold from where it is customary to seek out the nearest spring and so witness the birth of the river Lune, the minor eminences of Knoutberry and Knott retain higher ground as long as possible before declining green tracks offer an easy passage back to Town Head at the top end of the village.

St. Oswald's, Ravenstonedale

A Green Bell experience

right:
South to the adjoining Howgill Fells

bottom:
East to High Seat and Mallerstang Edge

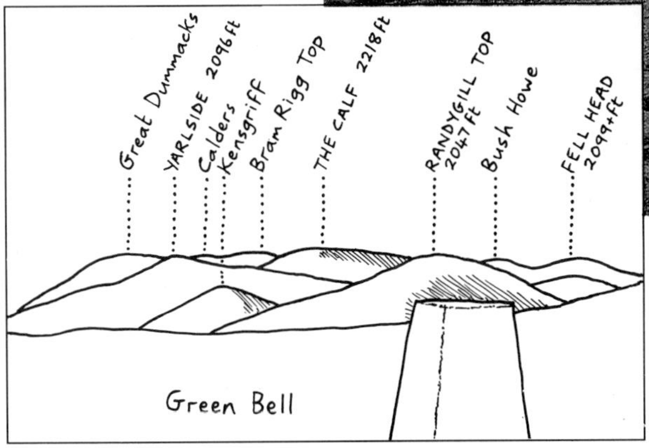

opposite, top:
Green Bell from Kensgriff

opposite, bottom:
West to Lakeland, with a skyline stretching from Coniston Old Man to Great Gable

CHAPTER FIVE SWALEDALE

WALK 24 COGDEN GILL & GRINTON MOOR 102

WALK 25 ARKENGARTHDALE 104

WALK 26 GREAT PINSEAT & OLD GANG MILL 107

WALK 27 GUNNERSIDE GILL 110

WALK 28 THE CORPSE ROAD & THE SWALE GORGE 113

WALK 29 AROUND KISDON HILL 116

Without taking a single thing away from its neighbours, this has got to be the finest of Yorkshire's Dales. Swaledale's isolation plays a part in its appeal, as for many of us (begging the pardon of its North-eastern devotees) it is the least accessible. Only after the length of Wharfedale or perhaps Ribblesdale and the interruption of Wensleydale do we come upon this promised land. This is a hidden valley, whether dropping into it from Tan Hill or Lamps Moss, the Buttertubs or Oxnop Head, Stang or Grinton Moor: unless working updale from its gateway town of Richmond, then you reach Swaledale the hard way.

Reeth is the walkers' capital, a base that caters well for all, and puts you in good heart even on a grey day. Somehow this valley, from its clusters of stone cottages and liberally dotted field-barns to its pockets of woodland and its summer meadows, seems a decade or two behind the rest. Despite the timelessness there's a workmanlike side to it, as the Swale rushes about its business and, outside of Reeth, its settlements crowd industriously together rather than lazing around a broad green as they might in Wensleydale.

Unsurpassed sweeps of heather carpet the moor-tops, while high mountains enclose the dalehead. Relentlessly steep valley sides and deep-carved gills are intermittently scarred by the remnants of a lead mining industry on which almost every family in the dale once relied, and the walker cannot go far without encountering a ravine-like hush or a ghostly smelt mill. Most of us could not imagine Swaledale without these features, nor the place-names such as Keld, Thwaite and Gunnerside, left by the norsemen who clearly felt at home here.

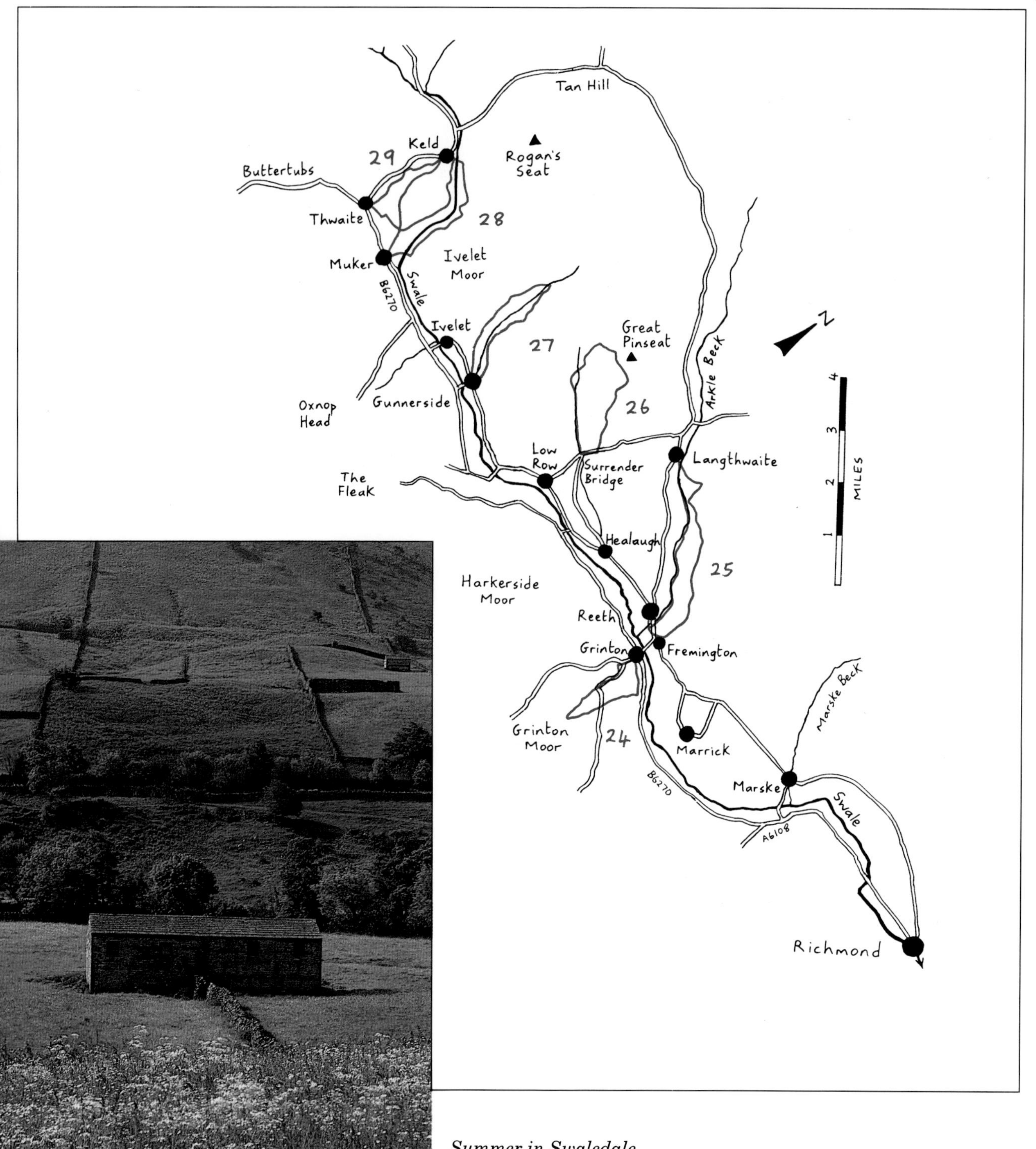

Summer in Swaledale

24: COGDEN GILL AND GRINTON MOOR

The flue climbing from Grinton Smelt Mill

Start: Grinton
Distance: 4 miles
Map: 1:25,000 - Yorkshire Dales North / Central
1:50,000 - Landranger 98

This steady jaunt only dips a toe into the sea of moorland amassed behind Grinton, but should whet the appetite sufficiently for the more meaty exertions that can readily be concocted. Of four roads leaving the village, the effort of choosing the one with the gradients soon reaps rewards, for the moor-edge quickly lends its grassy verges and outstanding views to the cause. Beyond castellated Grinton Lodge - a base for youth hostellers to roam the moors that were once the sole preserve of the gentry and their guests, who used the lodge for less wholesome moorland pleasures - the moor road runs along to cross Cogden Gill, and within minutes its bank will lead to the well preserved smelt mill that is the focal point of the walk.

Grinton Smelt Mill is the perfect objective for an evening stroll, when the ghostly buildings cast long shadows, and across the valley the finger of Arkengarthdale sinks into the dusk. Operative during the heady days of 19th century lead mining, its two buildings are a peat store and the smelting mill itself, while up the fellside the old flue runs straight as an arrow. Conspicuous by its absence is the chimney at

the flue top: its site, however, makes a fine vantage point before the walk resumes past the broken cliffs of Sharrow Hill and back to the road. A pleasant track proves a dependable guide down to Cogden Hall, with the surviving tower of Marrick Priory clearly visible across the Swale before returning to the village.

above:
Looking back over the smelt mill from the track onto the moor

right:
Grinton Lodge, looking to Fremington Edge

25: ARKENGARTHDALE

After the fashion of its parent valley, Arkengarthdale consists of huddled settlements that are legacies of lead mining days: miners' cottages blend into their settings while profuse scars of the old industry litter the heather moortops. Swaledale's breezy capital Reeth sits on a green table overseeing Arkle Beck's confluence with the Swale, exercising a flawless impartiality with its equal interest in Arkengarthdale. From a respectable distance the grey walls of Fremington Edge overlook Reeth's capacious green, and this lofty scarp is the first and most demanding objective upon leaving Reeth Bridge.

From Fremington a lane makes a start on the climb, becoming a rough track as it crawls past the conspicuous White House, by a quarry that won a flint known as chert, to eventual arrival on Fremington Edge. Striding out along the broad Edge Top, valley views are replaced by sweeping moorland panoramas until turning for the dale by way of Fell End Lead Mine. Features of the all-embracing Arkengarthdale views are the profile of Calver Hill opposite and the hamlet of Booze just across Slei Gill. At Strothwaite Hall on the valley floor a chance to shorten the walk makes for the beck, while the main route turns by the farm to relinquish its drive in favour of a stiff haul through the fields to Booze. From its almost forgotten buildings the humblest of roads winds down into Langthwaite.

above: A corner of Reeth

Start:	*Reeth*
Distance:	*9 miles*
Map:	*1:25,000 - Yorkshire Dales North / Central 1:50,000 - Landranger 92 & 98*

opposite, top:
Across Arkengarthdale to Calver Hill from Fremington Edge
opposite bottom:
Wall patterns at Castle Farm

Shop, church and inn firmly set Langthwaite up as the hub of the dale, while veterinary devotees will delight in recognising a familiar quaint arrangement. Also on offer is a two-mile extension to Eskeleth Bridge, up the side of the beck past the grandiose shooting lodge of Scar House, and back through the pastures opposite. Above the bridge is the powder house of the CB Smelt Mill, whose founder Charles Bathurst is commemorated in that most English of ways in a hostelry just up the road.

Return to Reeth begins with an extended Arkleside ramble that thrives on the unfrequented wooded corners and banks. On occasions the beck is abandoned - most notably in a pitifully derelict neighbourhood of crumbling walls and farm buildings - but estrangement is only ever temporary as a beckside flourish finally heralds the sighting of Reeth Bridge.

right:
Arkle Beck above Reeth
below:
Calver Hill forms a hazy backdrop to the meadows of Booze

26: GREAT PINSEAT AND OLD GANG MILL

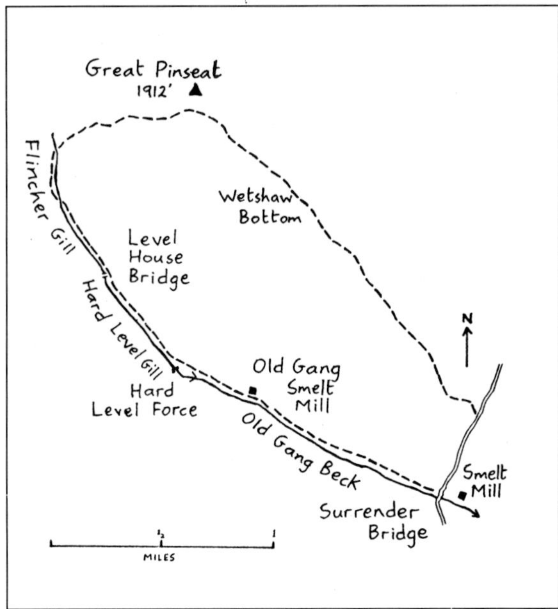

Start: *Surrender Bridge GR: 988998*
Distance: *$5^{3}/_{4}$ miles*
Map: *1:25,000 - Yorkshire Dales North / Central*
1:50,000 - Landranger 92 & 98 (just)

The marching line of the peat store, Old Gang

Only one of the great pleasures of open country is freedom from negotiating stiles, farmyards and intricate routes there-through, and no walk evades them better than this. The starting point itself is an isolated spot, high on the moors and ideally placed to cushion a climb to almost 2000 feet. The walk to the top of Great Pinseat would be hard pushed to be labelled an ascent, for from the road above Surrender Bridge a broad track makes an unbroken march, skirting the less than subtly named Wetshaw Bottom to come within a stone's throw of the top. Interest is provided by distant views, and curiosity aroused by the choice of this location for a long-abandoned delivery van from Reeth.

Such is Pinseat's girth that valleys are excluded from its wide prospects, and the aftermath of lead mining seems to occupy as much room as the moorland they were worked from. A white-painted O.S. column for once offers a rare brighter moment, and even then it hides behind a wall. Descent is quickly accomplished, and a prolonged tramp parallel with Hard Level Gill (or one of its aliases) leads all the way back to Surrender Bridge. This time, however, there is plenty to see, although one must be prepared for the

devastation left by lead mining to appreciate its qualities.

Hard Level Force lends itself as a natural attraction prior to arrival at the Old Gang Smelt Mill. The old place exudes an atmosphere that over-rides the years of decay, influenced heavily by the preserved chimney, and creditably work is in hand to conserve what remains. Ranged militarily across the skyline above are the remnants of the mill's peat store, while the Old Gang Mine itself is found at a higher level, some distance away across the valley. The line of a flue climbs the hillside behind the mill, though a better example can be seen at the end of the walk, now just a short mile downstream.

If by now absorbed in Swaledale's lead mining history, continue the few yards down from the bridge to inspect the Surrender Smelt Mill, from where its aforementioned flue can be seen marching up to a prominent chimney.

above:
Old Gang Smelt Mill

opposite:
Winter on Great Pinseat

bottom right:
The remains of Surrender Mill

27: GUNNERSIDE GILL

Start:
Gunnerside
Distance:
6 miles
Map:
1:25,000 - Yorkshire Dales North / Central
1:50,000 - Landranger 98 & either 91 or 92

Blakethwaite Smelt Mill

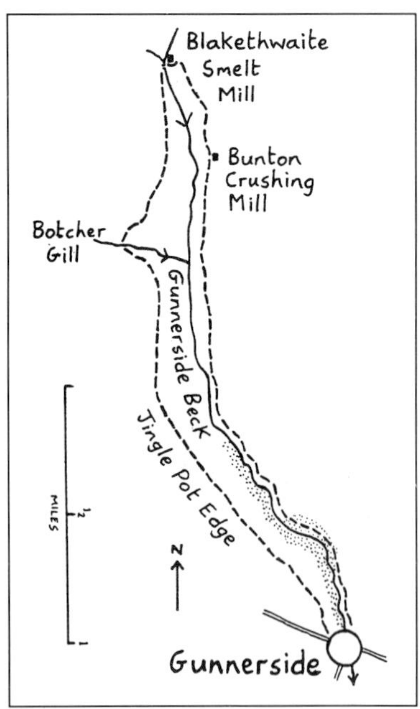

None of Swaledale's side valleys - arguably none in the entire Dales - drive so forcefully into their enclosing hillsides as that of Gunnerside Gill. Its key feature is the narrowness evident from its very foot, where Gunnerside itself guards an entrance past which only the foot-traveller can break through.

On my first visit a grey cloak was draped over the dale, and on leaving the vertical smoke-plumes of the lead miners' village, the eerie confines of the gill waited if not in menacing mood, then certainly oppressively. Level walking by the beck lead by dank tree-clad banks, and the following mile, while no more demanding, gave a clearer picture of what lay ahead. The first signs of long defunct lead workings were encountered at the crushing mill of the old Sir Francis Mine, and by the time I reached the stark remains of Bunton crushing mill the clinging mists gave clever camouflage to the scarred valley sides. Here were scattered ruins, dripping levels, spoil heaps and rubbly gashes where the miners' hushes had torn away vegetation in the search for workable veins.

Gunnerside Gill near the start of the walk

As I acclimatised to the gloom an appreciative feel for the place developed, and the dour inhospitality now seemed tailored to the surroundings to which the tentacles clung. A choice of beckside or higher level path brought me to the limit of my wanderings, the evocative tumbledown grouping at Blakethwaite Smelt Mill. Dominant feature is the peat store, its series of surviving arches adding a romantic touch to a workplace that would hold no such romanticism for its workforce.

In contrast to the much interrupted outward leg, the west side of the gill offered unbroken progress, commencing with a smooth green track slanting up through the last workings of the day. Paramount advantage, aside from permitting a speedy return, is its value as a terrace from which to make sense of the layout of the mining remains.

By now the mist was being prised from the hillsides, and the scale of the gill and all its trappings was overpowering after my near twilight experience. At Botcher Gill the way merged into a harsher shooters' track, and a long but rapid descent to Gunnerside was ideal escape from the vastly altered landscape of my morning's departure.

North Hush from Bunton Hush

Deep in Gunnerside Gill

28: THE CORPSE ROAD AND THE SWALE GORGE

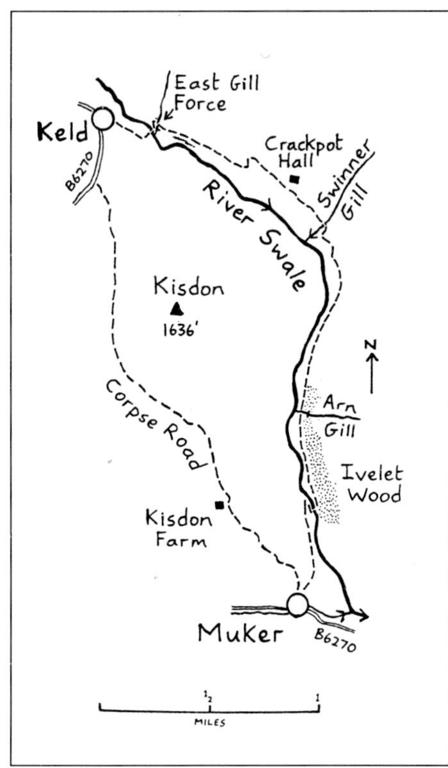

The hidden charm of Arngill Force

A precious few hours in Swaledale could not be put to better use than pulling on the boots and taking up this suggestion, for a walk that takes in Keld and Muker guarantees scenery of the highest order.

Start:
Muker
Distance:
6 miles
Map:
1:25,000 - Yorkshire Dales North / Central
1:50,000 - Landranger 91 & 98

right:
East Gill Force

below:
Looking down Swaledale from the Kisdon farm road

opposite:
On the Corpse Road above Keld

Upstream from Muker the Swale revels in its golden hour, away from roads and with 'nowt but scenery' to get in the way. A path makes a determined bee-line for the river by way of a series of gap-stiles through neatly packaged fields. Strategically sited Ramps Holme Bridge gives access to the opposite bank, from where a wide path rolls along the capacious flats of the valley floor. While unremitting flanks rise to both sides, they manage to form an enticing gangway rather than an intimidating tunnel. In the midst of all this grandeur, and easily missed, is the elysian setting of Arngill Force.

Wilder surroundings are reached as Swinner Gill is approached, the beck being crossed at the foot of what is an untamed ravine higher up, and can easily be visited from a path junction by Crackpot Hall. Climbing above the river, increasingly wooded country frames a terrace above craggy walls at the pulse of the Swale Gorge. On crossing East Gill the Pennine Way and the Coast to Coast Walk pass like ships in the night before a surprise appearance of the gem of East Gill Force immediately below. This is the only feature that these two renowned marathons share, an idyllic spot for the occasion. While any heavily laden trekkers will have many miles ahead of them, it is but a quarter-mile into Keld, just across the river.

The return leg is the historic route of a 'corpse road'. Many centuries ago when the church at Grinton served the entire dale, the dead had to be transported the length of the valley for burial, and this crossing of Kisdon Hill was merely the first stage. To this day it remains the most direct route between Keld and Muker, though happily the motor road takes a less obtrusive course. A further advantage of the old road is the sweeping vistas it reveals, first across to the bulging walls and carefree heights of Lovely Seat and Great Shunner Fell; then during descent the green floor of the dale is seen stretching far beyond Muker's fair setting. Between isolated Kisdon Farm and Cottage the Pennine Way is crossed for the second time, and soon the jumbled but compact village of Muker is extending its hospitality.

29: AROUND KISDON HILL

Start:
Keld
Distance:
$5^{1/2}$ miles
Map:
1:25,000 - Yorkshire Dales North / Central
1:50,000 - Landranger 98 & either 91 or 92

The ravine of Swinnergill from the path below North Gang Scar

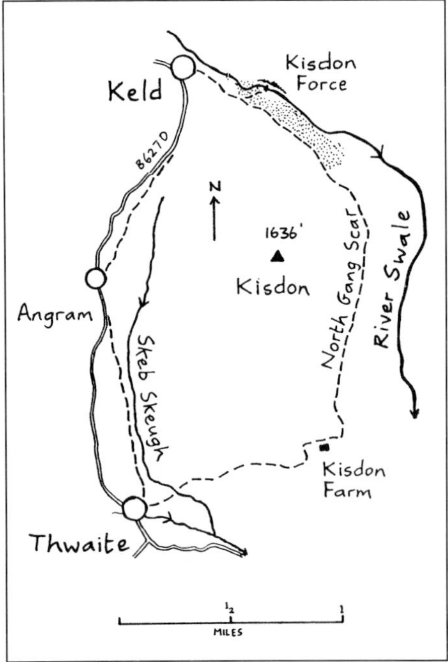

Though its ascent is unheard of, Kisdon Hill throws down uniform slopes that are trodden by thousands of walkers every year, and this walk contrasts a stroll along its western base with an unforgettable traverse high along its eastern flank, thereby encircling the hill entirely on its own territory.

The first section saunters along undemanding field-paths linking the farming corner of Angram with better known Keld and Thwaite, themselves little more than hamlets but favourites of ramblers far beyond the bounds of the Yorkshire Dales. Despite lacking height, the path yields fine views of this wild

right: *Kisdon Force*
below: *Kisdon from across the Swale - the terrace path is clearly evident high on its flanks*

corner of the upper dale. Though the valley road runs through this broad divide in the hills, note that for once it does not shadow the river, for alongside is nothing more than a stream with the curious name of Skeb Skeugh. Instead, the Ice Age saw the Swale breaking through the neck of land holding Kisdon Hill, to carve the incisive course soon to be displayed.

Thwaite assumes a cosy slot under Kisdon, and a much vaunted tearoom waylays many a walker before resuming his travels. Negotiating a way through its back yards, the Pennine Way makes a short climb up the heathery southern end of Kisdon to lonely Kisdon

left:
The warmth of summer at Keld
below:
The first snows of winter at Thwaite

Farm. Here the path selects a shelf along the wall of Kisdon, and while the famous PW may have bigger individual moments, this is arguably its finest hour. Running along a limestone terrace below the line of North Gang Scar, it is the perfect promenade for appraising the Swale's grandest reach, with the ravine of Swinner Gill excellently displayed across the dale. Such grandeur can scarcely be contained in the frame of a mere photograph.

On dropping into the wooded confines of the Swale Gorge proper, and with Keld but a whisper away, an essential detour awaits: turn to the river to witness Kisdon Force pouring over a narrow ledge, between abundant foliage in an inspiring setting - a spectacular conclusion to any walk.

On the path under North Gang Scar, looking across the Swale to Rogan's Seat

CHAPTER SIX WENSLEYDALE

WALK 30 AYSGARTH FALLS & CASTLE BOLTON 122

WALK 31 NAPPA HALL & ASKRIGG'S FALLS 125

WALK 32 AROUND ADDLEBROUGH 128

WALK 33 SEMERWATER & THE ROMAN ROAD 131

WALK 34 HARDRAW FORCE & HIGH CLINT 134

WALK 35 HELL GILL & THE HIGH WAY 137

Wensleydale could not contrast more with its parallel colleague Swaledale. This is a broad green dale that calls for greater exploration in order to discover its subtle charms. Its villages may be obvious enough - and in West Burton, Askrigg and Bainbridge it can match anything - but so much is hidden here, and this is where the walker scores heavily over the general visitor. Another difference is the proliferation of side-valleys, from the long, lonely miles of Coverdale to the quiet charm of Walden, Bishopdale and Widdale. Favourite of many is that of the river Bain, which contains that rare creature the Dales' lake.

Probably Wensleydale's greatest asset is its incomparable array of waterfalls, though curiously the Ure itself offers little outside of its playfulness at Aysgarth. Again, we are down to seeking out these furtive creatures - either on the sizeable side becks or the short-lived gills. Historic connections are generally few and far between in upland areas, yet Wensleydale will show you a Roman fort, an abbey, a castle, and a fortified manor house along with something from just about every century. Little obviously dramatic scenery here perhaps, but don't dismiss Wensleydale as a land of fat cows in green fields.

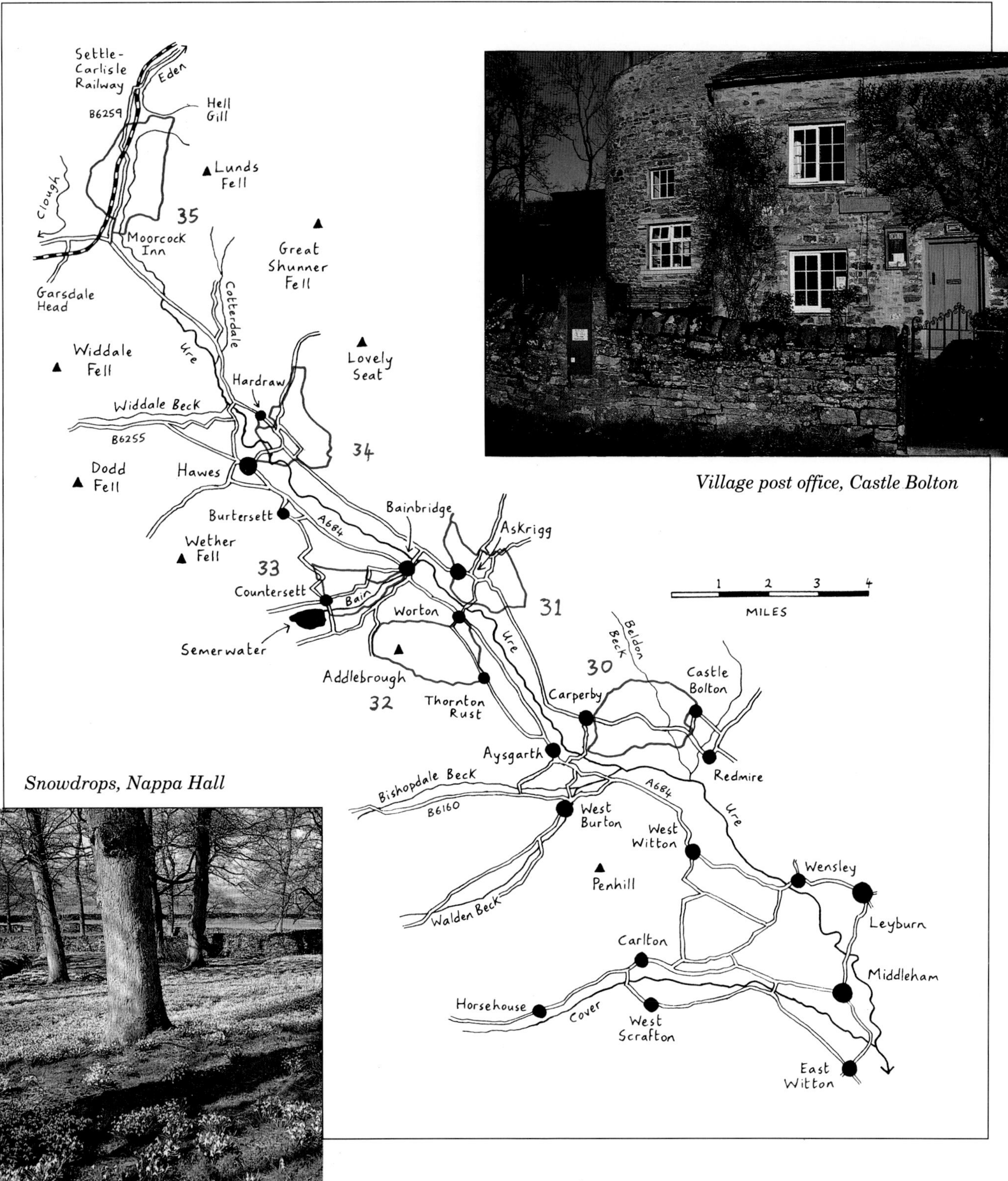

Village post office, Castle Bolton

Snowdrops, Nappa Hall

30: AYSGARTH FALLS AND CASTLE BOLTON

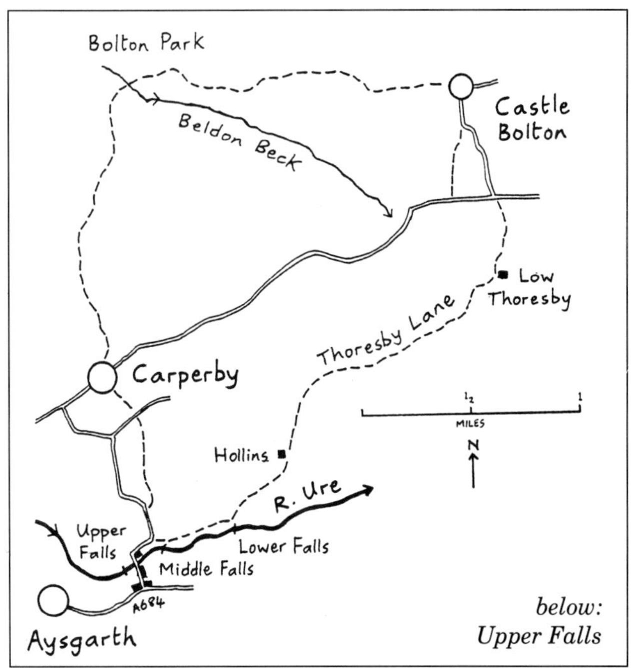

below: Upper Falls

Each extremity of this walk boasts one of the Dales' outstanding landmarks, major tourist attractions that will be better appreciated in their settings after a cross-country approach. These moments are only the icing on the cake, however, in a journey that spreads itself over a great diversity of landscapes.

Curious glances from falls-bound trippers marked my departure from Aysgarth Falls car park, as I chose to pass under an arch of the torn-up track of the Wensleydale Railway. Past the spectre of Aysgarth's station a brief foray into Freeholder's Wood in which the walk would end was the gateway to a maze of limestone walls bisected by gapstiles, a refreshing change from the cumbersome ladders that have replaced so many of these works of art. Emerging opposite the inn at Carperby, a plaque proclaimed its location as Herriot's honeymoon hotel, while another warned of the presence of Websters beers. I'll warrant the young vet didn't face that prospect at the bar.

Up Hargill the road became a rough track, and ultimately a green baize way as long strides covered the colourful vastness of Bolton Park: higher still were the grouse moors bordering Swaledale. The pile of Bolton Castle had been in my sights for a full two miles before being deposited under its prepossessing walls. Its four-square appearance in lower Wensleydale scenes serves to underline its powerful hold over the two lines of cottages at its feet that constitute Castle Bolton.

The castle was, perhaps surprisingly, built during the late 14th century as a grandiose residence rather than a fortress, and was the pride of many generations of the Scrope family. It later passed to the Lords Bolton, and has recently been undergoing major renovation in order to arrest further decay and also to make as much of it as possible available for public inspection. Though it saw its share of Civil War action during a year-long siege, it is probably best known for the six months it kept Mary, Queen of Scots under lock and key.

A couple below the castle wall were casting puzzled looks over a walking guide as I hastened past to cross the railway again in a low cutting that gave only a taste of the wonderful journey it offered. A leafy snicket was again only an appetiser for what lay in store, where Low Thoresby Farm held the key to one of the finest of green lanes. What sets Thoresby Lane apart from most of its kind is the first magical half-mile being of such slender proportions as to be only pedestrian-friendly: even the horse-rider or cyclist would find it a touch uncomfortable. It is heartily reassuring to find a green lane out of bounds to the growing band of undesirables for whom the hundreds of thousands of miles of tarmac already burying our land are insufficient. Like a fairground ride my way wound mysteriously by pastures I couldn't see, such was the exhuberance of hedgerows that channelled me faithfully through to daylight. Before emerging, a virgin bridleway branched off to ford the Ure: its title of Watery Lane left nothing to the imagination.

The unbroken wall of Penhill occupied me as the immediate vicinity returned to cows in green fields, and at Hollin House the piles of honest muck were soon forgotten as my ears detected the roar of the Ure. Aysgarth's Lower Falls were indeed soon on display, a cleft in the rock wall that lines the river affording an immediate opportunity to admire the cascading waters before shadowing the bank up to the more conventional viewpoint. In the company of waterfall collectors a carpet of beechnut husks transported me through timeless woodland to a similar vantage point for the Middle Falls. Only the upper third of Aysgarth's pride and joy remained, though these rapids could just be viewed from the car on the way home!

Start:	*Aysgarth*
Distance:	*7 miles*
Map:	*1:25,000 - Yorkshire Dales North / Central*
	1:50,000 - Landranger 98

right: Bolton Castle
top: St. Andrew's, Aysgarth

overleaf: Middle Falls, Aysgarth

31: NAPPA HALL AND ASKRIGG'S FALLS

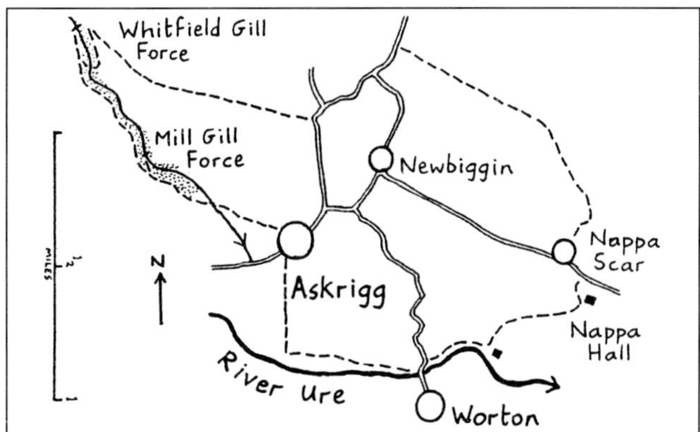

Setting out on this ramble unaware of the delights in store, the humble traveller will surely return to Askrigg in a state of euphoria. Aside from other attractions, either one of the brace of waterfalls behind the village would in itself be justification for undertaking this journey: as long as nobody discloses these wonders to the multitude at Aysgarth!

This subtle approach to the falls saves their splendour for the latter stages, so for now head for the river, to a typically unflappable Ure far removed from the rough and tumble of its tributaries. Departure from the valley floor finds you at an archway framing the battlemented Nappa Hall: still very much in use as a farm, it dates from the 15th century when it served as a fortified manor house of the powerful Metcalfe family. A walker passing through at the dawning of springtime will have his visit long etched in his memory by the display depicted on page 121.

High above this quiet corner of the dale a superb green lane runs below Ellerkin Scar, enjoying very much an archetypal Wensleydale scene: parcelled fields with their liberally scattered barns lead the eye over the dale to Addlebrough and a build-up of higher ground further west. Winding through a network of lanes, the mile-long Low Straights Lane is key to the comprehensively wooded inner sanctum of Whitfield Gill and all that lies therein.

Mill Gill Force

Start: *Askrigg*
Distance: *7 miles*
Map: *1:25,000 - Yorkshire Dales North / Central*
1:50,000 - Landranger 98

At the culmination of this rough lane Whitfield Gill Force signals its presence through the trees, but it is necessary to turn downstream to cross the beck and double back. The cul-de-sac path knows its goal, and after a little slithering, halts at the impasse created by the unbroken plunge and the arena into which it pours. Retracing steps the beck undergoes a name-change in readiness for its second great feat, and a similar but less demanding path again turns back to claim an equally suitable pedestal for Mill Gill Force. Its great asset is that despite a similarly appointed ravine, its tiered cascades ensure this is no mere repetition of its higher neighbour.

All that remains is to shadow the beck down to a mill it once powered, and the timeless streets of Askrigg are almost underfoot. Its immeasureable charm is on open display, from the market cross by the 15th century church to its elegant three-storeyed houses.

above left:
Nappa Hall
above:
Across the dale to Addlebrough from the green lane above Nappa Scar
opposite:
Whitfield Gill Force, and a spring rainbow

32: AROUND ADDLEBROUGH

Semerwater from the scarp on Addlebrough

In Wensleydale altitude counts for nowt, for Addlebrough and Penhill are its proud sons, not the 2000-footers hiding behind their decorative skirts. Addlebrough has the dubious distinction of not possessing a right of way to its summit, but this circuit of the fell passes sufficiently near the top to allow keener types to strike off for higher ground.

The sleepy hamlet of Worton sees a road climb through the long, low scar that parades along the side of the dale, and from the farming corner of Cubeck the way constantly improves from rough lane to broad green swath, as Addlebrough's summit comes into view from a plateau in its lap. Being deposited on a narrow road is less of a surprise than the view it furnishes, for directly below, the blue sheet of Semerwater basks in its bowl of rolling hills.

The road ends at Carpley Green, though this old pack-way roams on to the heights of the Stake and ultimately upper Wharfedale. By now the cut-away profile of Addlebrough demands attention, and so it is

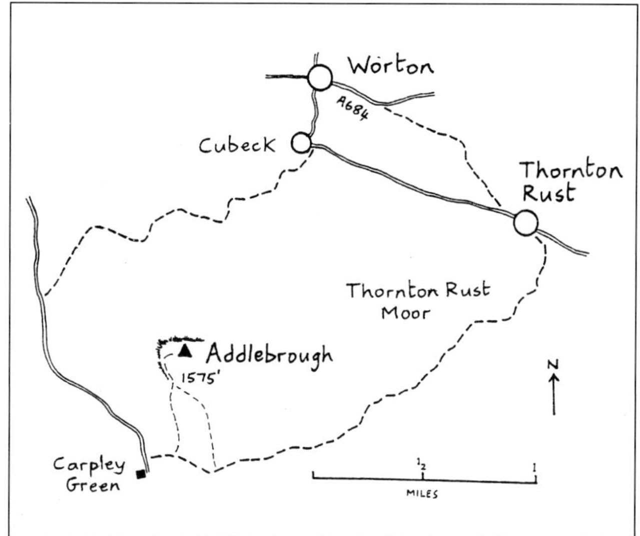

top:
Autumn sunlight breaks through the woodland below Thornton Rust

right:
Addlebrough from Semerwater

Start:
Worton
Distance:
6½ miles
Map:
1:25,000 - Yorkshire Dales North / Central
1:50,000 - Landranger 98

Snow-capped Addlebrough dominates mid-Wensleydale

that another bridleway strikes off through the gap behind it. If the scars up to the left prove too inviting, then gravitate towards them to improve the picture of Semerwater valley and the whole of upper Wensleydale. This lofty perch reveals the outline of an ancient Iron-age settlement of the Brigante tribe on a shelf below, offering a prospect usually reserved for birds of the air. By now the Ordnance column and the dark northern edge are but a minute over the wall, and a way has been made near the acute corner of the scarp, where piles of stones form a makeshift stile in a section of fence.

Back on the bridleway, tamer but more open country awaits the route as it raises itself to a high quality green track to engage the undulations of Thornton Rust Moor. In time it falls to the charming village of that name sitting high above the valley, escaping the busy road but enjoying the benefits of the bus service. The walk concludes with its only true field-path, first exploring a finger of woodland before the game of seeking out the next Worton-bound gapstile. Final points of interest are some sights across the river, notably the castellated tower of Nappa Hall and slanting Ivy Scar above Woodhall.

Archetypal Wensleydale country on the final stage of the walk (with Nappa Hall discernible across the dale)

33: SEMERWATER AND THE ROMAN ROAD

Start:
Bainbridge
Distance:
5¾ miles
Map:
1:25,000 - Yorkshire Dales North / Central
1:50,000 - Landranger 98

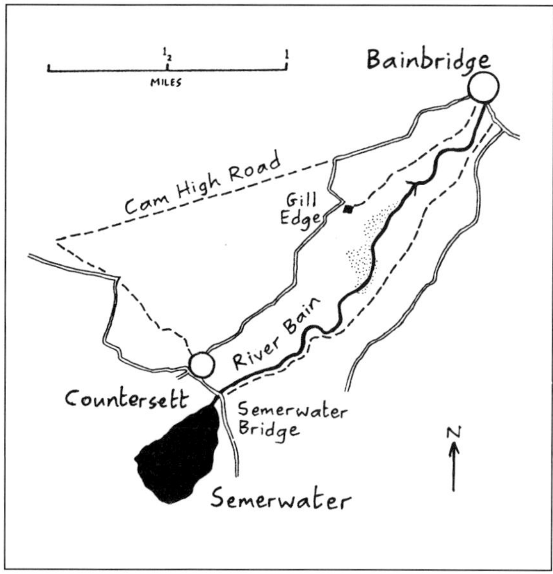

Quiet day at Semerwater

The river Bain on the way out, the Roman road on the way back, and Semerwater in between: this simple concept results in a varied walk south of Bainbridge. The Bain is traced for 2 of its modest 2½ miles, and from the 'Bain' Bridge in the village make an early halt to peer into its waters, for this playful descent over a series of ledges is its finest moment. The walk to Semerwater Bridge is a two-halved affair: firstly climbing above the river's deep trough to survey its setting (and claim an early sighting of the lake) then latching on to shadow its reedy bank through green pastures to its exit from Semerwater.

Out of season visits earn space to potter about the foreshore of the North Riding's largest natural lake, which has certainly seen life if legends have a say. Beneath the still waters an entire city was submerged after its poor welcome incurred a traveller's wrath, while on the shore sits the Carlow Stone, dropped by a passing giant, or perhaps the Devil. Rather more credibility can be attached to the theory that Iron-age folk erected lake-dwellings here. Whatever, only the boulder remains to witness man's present day exploits, the inevitable water sports. If Semerwater's appeal is matched by a surfeit of time

The Carlow Stone on the lakeshore

and energy, then a tidy circuit can be made by way of footpath to Stalling Busk's old church, track to Marsett, and quiet road back to Countersett, adding a little under four miles and giving a thorough insight into Semerwater and its valley.

The climb to the Roman road is bisected at Countersett, early Quaker connections evident in its Friends' Meeting House and Old Hall, wrapped up in its cottage neighbours. Known as the Cam High Road, the Romans' highway to Bainbridge from Ingleton was treated respectfully at the time of the enclosures by the addition of broadly spaced walls, and along with the vanished forests it is the network of stone walls that would today cause most wonder to the ghost of a legionary.

The Old Hall, Countersett

As it descends from the near 2000ft contour it has courted for many a lonely mile, the road affords uninterrupted vistas over Wensleydale's plump greenery, and aside from our leisure pursuits, it retains its usefulness for such tasks as the droving of sheep from higher pastures. The last leg into Bainbridge and their fort has been adapted for motors, but branching off to Gill Edge gives a more deserving finish through fields above the Bain.

right:
The River Bain below Semerwater
below:
Rose and Crown, Bainbridge

34: HARDRAW FORCE AND HIGH CLINT

While the high mountains encircling upper Wensleydale stand aloof from the life of the valley, their flanks act as intermediary for the walker. Finest example of this is the escarpment of High Clint above Sedbusk, which at 1700ft claims a generous altitude for a survey of the upper dale without demanding the rigours associated with its laid-back parent fell Lovely Seat.

Start:	*Hawes*
Distance:	*7¼ miles*
Map:	*1:25,000 - Yorkshire Dales North / Central*
	1:50,000 - Landranger 98

left:
The beacons on Pike Hill, looking to the dale head

opposite:
Hardraw Force in the grip of winter

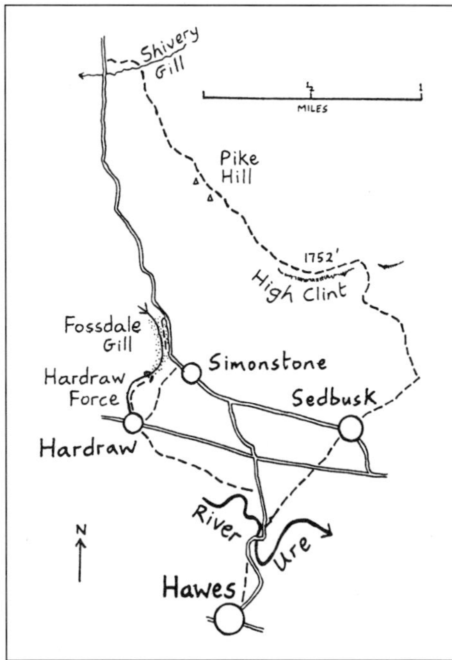

Pleasant field-paths link Hawes and Sedbusk, crossing the Ure at the arches of Haylands Bridge, and allowing time to eye up the scar which breaks the skyline ahead. Past Sedbusk's few cottages, escape from a rough lane brings an agreeable green way into play to climb to the increasingly prominent limestone bastion. Rarely does the Yoredale limestone of Wensleydale gleam like its carboniferous cousins of Craven, but on the commanding rim of High Clint it is positively resplendent.

A long promenade leads on to the upstanding beacons of Pike Hill, where a close-knit family and further, more distant, cousins forever stare across to the bulky heights planted in the heart of the Dales. Beyond here the limestone shrinks away, and the mini-ravine of Shivery Gill is the signal to drop down to the Buttertubs road bound for Swaledale. A long downhill mile to High Shaw brings a chance to get acquainted with the wooded charm of Fossdale Gill as it trains for its very special moment.

Another field-path runs from Simonstone down to Hardraw, where the detour to the famous force awaits. Even those who never darken the door of a public house will be prepared to break a vow on this occasion, for admission to the private grounds of the waterfall is through the Green Dragon Inn. It is but a five minute walk into the intimidating bowl of Hardraw Scaur, a natural amphitheatre recognised as such by the presence of a bandstand where revived contests flourish. Although the flow of water may be meagre, the nature of the unbroken 100ft fall is sufficient to guarantee favourable reaction. Back in the hamlet the walk is concluded as it began, with a flagged path running through the fields to Haylands Bridge.

above:
Pike Hill from across the dale near Gayle (note the prominent line of spoil from the old stone mines)
right:
Limekiln under High Clint

35: HELL GILL AND THE HIGH WAY

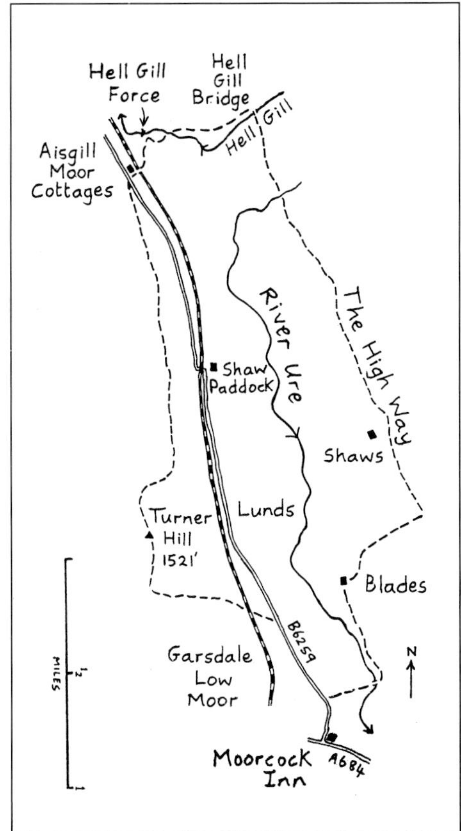

Hell Gill Force

Start:
Moorcock Inn GR: 797926
Distance:
7¼ miles
Map:
1:25,000 - Pathfinder 617 (SD69/79) & 608 (NY80/SD89) (tiny portion)
1:50,000 - Landranger 98

While Wensleydale echoes to singing waters, the river itself, other than at the obvious places, travels a restrained course. This expedition seeks excitement however in the very infant murmurings of the Ure, and proceeds to find a superb waterfall in the headwaters of the river Eden.

More than a thousand feet up, the Moorcock Inn is strategically sited at a junction of roads to the small country towns of Hawes, Sedbergh and Kirkby Stephen, and relies heavily on the trade of travellers between them. All around are sombre hillsides in a dozen shades of brown, and though they promise little, they give a creditable return on a three-hour investment.

above: The Moorcock Inn

below: Approaching Hell Gill on the High Way, with the grandeur of Wild Boar Fell as a backdrop

Tracks through lower pastures lead over the youthful Ure and by the colourful farm of Blades to climb to the High Way. Once the main route between Kirkby Stephen and Hawes, it now provides discerning walkers with a marvellous terrace between the upper reaches of the great rivers Ure and Eden. It is best known for its links with Lady Anne Clifford, who came this way from Skipton when doing the rounds of her clutch of Westmerian castles.

Interestingly, in view of the starting point, the Way is actually picked up at derelict High Dyke, a travellers' inn long ago. Turning along the old road a couple of miles of gradient-free marching await, with ample scope for looking beyond the Settle-Carlisle Line to the sharp profile of Wild Boar Fell and its less extrovert partner Swarth Fell.

The Ure is next stumbled upon at a ravine below the path, showing its first signs of activity after an unpublicised birth higher up the slopes of Lunds Fell.

top: *On Dandrymire Viaduct, Garsdale Head*
bottom: *Wild Boar Fell from Hell Gill Force*

The gorge is worth a little exploration, being more accessible than the more celebrated ravine that lies ahead. Within half a mile the High Way crosses, imperceptibly, the watershed of England, and in some style. Hell Gill Bridge spans the mysterious, slender canyon of Hell Gill, scoured by the beck that gives the Eden the best of christening presents. This auspicious start may seem out of character for a river better known for its sweeping course through a fertile vale, but there is more to come upon dropping down to witness the impact of the plunge of Hell Gill Force. Passengers on the adjacent railway are also treated to this splendid display, though they must remain alert to steal their glimpse.

From waters heading for the Solway turn to renew allegiance with the Ure, which will see the oceans by way of the Humber's mouth. At Aisgill Moor Cottages railway and road are crossed - the former just past its record-breaking 1169ft summit - for a less spectacular return leg. Wild scenery remains, however, as flanks rise to the rounded top of Turner Hill, where the piercing February winds encouraged the metal gatepost to render an acceptable imitation of a steel band.

To the right is the hidden valley of Grisedale, known by many through a 1970s documentary 'The Dale That Died', though familiar to very few in the raw. Life still forges on in this upland enclave, but only tentatively in an unyielding landscape where the winters take some shifting. Pastures long gone to seed are predominant on this walk, and the final one leads down to the railway yielding majestic views across to Mallerstang Edge and deep into the cleft of Wensleydale proper. The line is re-crossed by a high footbridge, a useful viewing platform if a train should be approaching.

CHAPTER SEVEN **NIDDERDALE**

WALK 36 BRIMHAM ROCKS & FELL BECK 142

WALK 37 RAVEN'S GILL & GUISE CLIFF 144

WALK 38 WATH & THE NIDD 148

WALK 39 FOUNTAINS EARTH MOOR 151

WALK 40 SCAR HOUSE & DALE EDGE 154

This is probably the strangest omission from the Dales Park, for unlike the ill-treated areas on the western bounds, Nidderdale was in possession of a valid passport, i.e. membership of the county of Yorkshire. This travesty stems from so much of the land being held by a water authority, and its high moors being jealously guarded as grouse shooting territory. Only now, decades later, are the Nidderdale Moors finally looking to see recognition as an Area of Outstanding Natural Beauty.

Pateley Bridge is the beating heart of Nidderdale, a workaday little town that saw first trains and then buses head for the updale communities, today leaving us to fend for ourselves. Ramsgill, Lofthouse and Middlesmoor are the triumvirate of upper Nidderdale villages, split from the lower dale by the elongated waters of Gouthwaite Reservoir, yet themselves some miles from the dalehead. At Lofthouse a water authority toll road on the track of the railway that helped build the dalehead reservoirs takes over for the remaining miles to Scar House, and here, beyond the last of the farms, is arguably the bleakest of Yorkshire's dale ends. Below Pateley there is little change, other than high on the hillside where the natural wonderland of Brimham Rocks justifiably attains celebrity status.

Be it the lack of National Park attention or dearth of glamorous attractions, there can be little doubt that Nidderdale is well off the beaten track, and it doesn't seem to be complaining.

Gouthwaite Reservoir

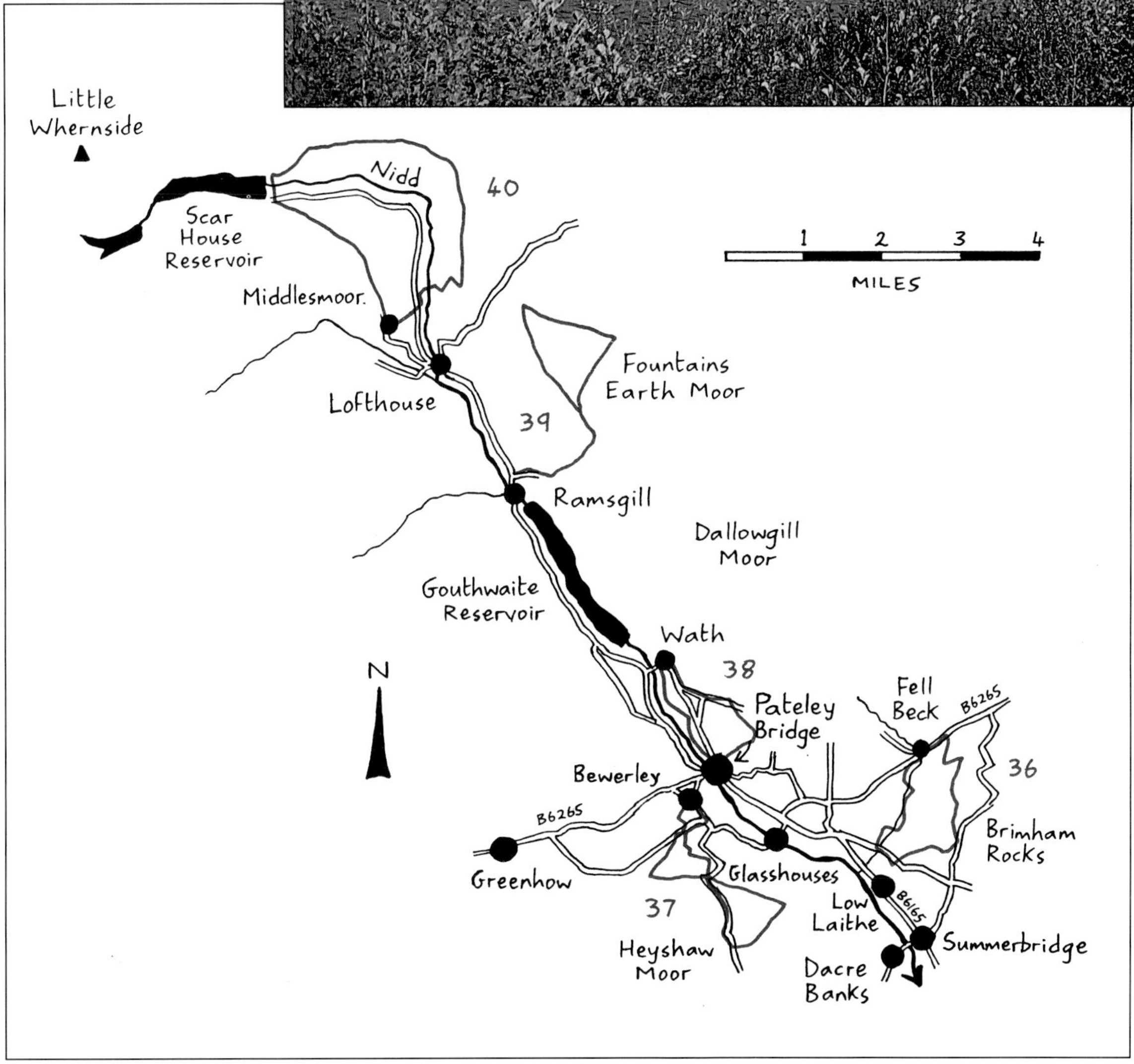

Little Whernside
Nidd
40
Scar House Reservoir
1 2 3 4
MILES
Middlesmoor.
Fountains Earth Moor
Lofthouse
39
Ramsgill
Dallowgill Moor
Gouthwaite Reservoir
Wath
38
N
Pateley Bridge
Fell Beck
B6265
36
Bewerley
B6265
Brimham Rocks
Greenhow
Glasshouses
Low Laithe
B6165
37
Summerbridge
Heyshaw Moor
Dacre Banks

36: BRIMHAM ROCKS AND FELL BECK

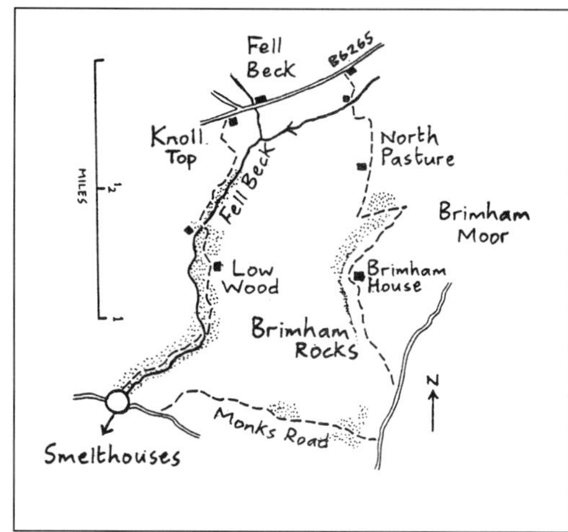

There's always one isn't there?

The natural playground of Brimham Rocks is the showpiece of Nidderdale, and is many tourists' only acquaintance with the valley. The 50-odd acres of bizarrely sculpted outcrops form a jagged skyline from below, and indeed the valley approach is the most fulfilling. The hamlet of Smelthouses is ideally placed, but as it lends little space to leave a vehicle, the Rocks' car park is likely to be most practicable. The disadvantage is that unless reversing the walk, the rocks are first on the agenda, rather than a goal for which to aim. Two obvious lines link the environs of Brimham Rocks and Smelthouses, and the wooded gill of Fell Beck and a well preserved monks' trod combine neatly for this purpose.

Assuming a start from the Rocks, then one way of saving their thousand and one nooks and crannies is to take the broad drive to the Rocks House, once a keeper's house, and now a visitor centre with the usual National Trust aromas. Beyond it more outcrops - including some of the easier recognised 'named' rocks - can be found before crossing the moor to leave the drama and the crowds behind, for now. Simple pastures are the order of the day as far as the neighbourhood of Fell Beck hamlet, before reticent paths lead into Fell Beck's wooded dells. Exquisite tracts of woodland - great swaths of birch being particularly in evidence - usher the path nimbly downstream to the select residences of Smelthouses.

As its name suggests this was once the site of mills for smelting ore from the Yorke family's mines in the district, and some of today's dwellings have seen conversion from industrial use. The climb back to the Rocks begins almost at once on the other side of the beck, and at this point the gnarled 'Rocks' skyline invokes its magnetic pull. This is no ordinary rural ramble, however, for throughout its entire length back to the heathery caresses of Brimham Moor the route treads a magically preserved green way used by monks en route to and from their great Cistercian house at Fountains, only five miles distant. Unviolated by motorised traffic, this enclosed byway is a linear nature trail, and an absolute joy to tread.

On the uplifting expanse of Brimham Moor it is but minutes to the car park, so at the first opportunity break off the moor road and get down to the serious business of exploring!

Start:
Brimham Rocks
Distance:
$5^{1}/_{2}$ miles
Map: 1:25,000 -
Pathfinder 652 (SE16)
& 653 (SE26/36)
1:50,000 - Landranger 99

The magical playground of Brimham

The Idol Rock

37: RAVEN'S GILL AND GUISE CLIFF

left:
Yorke's Folly
below:
Among the boulders of High Crag Ridge

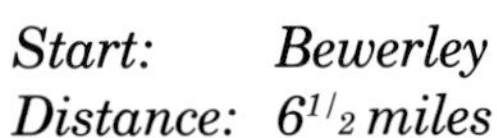

Start:	*Bewerley*
Distance:	*6 1/2 miles*
Map:	*1:25,000 - Pathfinder 652 (SE16)*
	1:50,000 - Landranger 99

A veritable embarrassment of riches illuminates the moorland south of Pateley Bridge, downdale of which one might have expected tamer country to move in.

Certain walks demand circuitous routes, and on this occasion a figure-of-eight - centred on Yorke's Folly - effectively bisects it: as the two halves are essentially complementary, however, only the complete journey will capture the full spirit of Bewerley's hinterland.

Pateley Bridge's exclusive sidekick Bewerley sees you off through the ornamental charm of Fishpond Wood to reach the foot of Skrikes Wood, to be enjoyed at the end of the walk. For now it is a steep pull to Raven's Nest Farm, perched on a broad ridge above the deeply carved Raven's Gill. A shooters' track offers to fire you onto the broad acres of Flat Moor, but the twin towers of Yorke's Folly beckon like the road to Wembley. Down in the confines of the gill a redundant sheepfold flounders in bracken, while the playful beck splashes over a ledge in surroundings that waylay all but the blinkered.

above:
Nidderdale from Guise Cliff - in evidence are the marquees of the valley's big day of the year, at Pateley

right:
Autumn tapestry - Fishpond Wood from Skrikes Wood

Intermittent trods skirt gritstone outcrops to the top of the road up Nought Bank, and from this popular motorists' halt Yorke's Folly is but two minutes' scamper. 200 years ago, in the eccentric manner of the upper crust, one of Nidderdale's Yorke family gave local men valuable employment with the construction of a ruin, no less. The two free-standing pillars have mourned their third member since it fell prey to violent storms a century ago, but the survivors seem capable of attracting visitors for a long time yet.

At this point magnificent Guise Cliff begins to take shape, and is reached along a moor-edge path that cannot begin to prepare you for the cliff-top promenade that follows. Although the main path refrains from venturing too near the edge, a tangle of adventurous trods tempt stray feet to the brink of alarming precipices. With caution those with a head

above:
Looking out over Guisecliff Wood from Guise Cliff
right:
Yorke's Folly pricks the skyline from across the Nidd

opposite:
In Raven's Gill

for such dizzy heights can gaze down in awe from a dramatic stance, though heather-masked clefts await the unwary. The view, which included Brimham Rocks, Pateley Bridge, Gouthwaite Reservoir and the high moors of the dalehead, is enhanced by the broccoli-head carpet of Guisecliff Wood, which in spite of its saturation coverage is unlikely to be of value as a safety net.

The scattered boulders of High Crag Ridge break up the crossing to Heyshaw Moor, then it's back down the moorland road to familiar ground. After paying homage to the gaping jaws of the Crocodile Rock, a descent through Skrikes Wood nature reserve leads back to the foot of Raven's Gill. On re-entering Bewerley, the secretive chapel of Bewerley Grange (restored from its 15th century origins) merits a silent moment of prayer, if only for the chance to have been enriched by this wonderful outdoor experience.

38: WATH AND THE NIDD

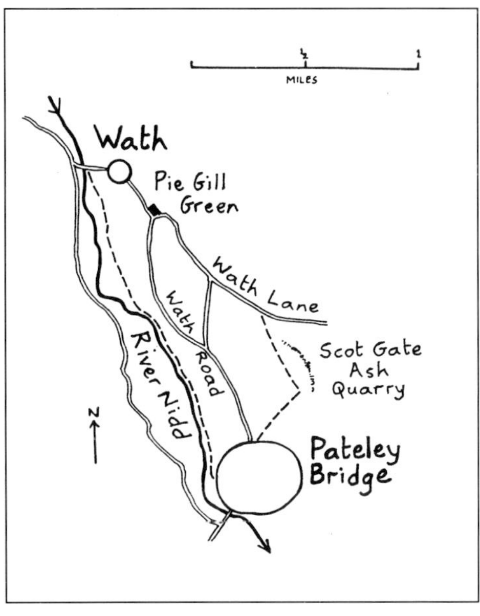

Autumn by the Nidd, near Pateley Bridge

Start:
Pateley Bridge
Distance:
4 miles
Map:
1:25,000 -
Pathfinder 652 (SE16)
1:50,000 - Landranger 99

Man's industrial influence on one small rural area could not be better portrayed than here, where on the edge of an old market town, forestry, quarrying, a light railway, an incline tramway, a reservoir, and more distantly lead mining are observed. All that remains of the railways are grassy embankments amongst the fields, more than sufficient to fire the imagination.

The two enterprising lines met a third, conventional one at long-abandoned Pateley Bridge station, and here, by the foot of the main street, the trail begins. The only effort involved is soon embraced, for from the Wath road the ever-steepening course of the tramway climbs high above the town to the scene of devastation that was, until relatively recently, Scot Gate Ash Quarry. On this extensive site the strong delphstone was excavated, to be lowered 600 feet to waiting railway waggons.

Free of the chaotic scene, one can take in a more verdant landscape in which green fields lead the eye to the waters of Gouthwaite Reservoir. This was Bradford's first attempt at damming the valley, and it must be acknowledged the finger-like sheet blends harmoniously into its setting, more so than the soulless plantations above its shore. There is a certain irony in the fact that the pastures drowned by Gouthwaite Reservoir were only 'temporarily' occupying the bed of a glacial lake, just waiting for the waters to return. Across the dale are sites of intensive lead mining high on Ashfold Side and Bewerley Moor.

West Riding remembered in sleepy Nidderdale

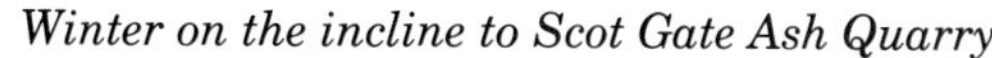

Winter on the incline to Scot Gate Ash Quarry

Grass verges ease the way down to the sequestered hamlet of Wath, where the inn sign captures a favourite means of recreation in the upper dale. A restored station house gives a clue to the return leg, which enjoys a march along the track-bed of the Nidd Valley Light Railway, constructed in 1908 to serve reservoir construction at the dalehead. When the Nidd stops its meanderings and learns to follow suit, latch onto its direct, tree-lined course - all change at Pateley Bridge!

Springtime on the banks of the Nidd

Summer above Pie Gill Green, looking over Wath to Gouthwaite Reservoir

39: FOUNTAINS EARTH MOOR

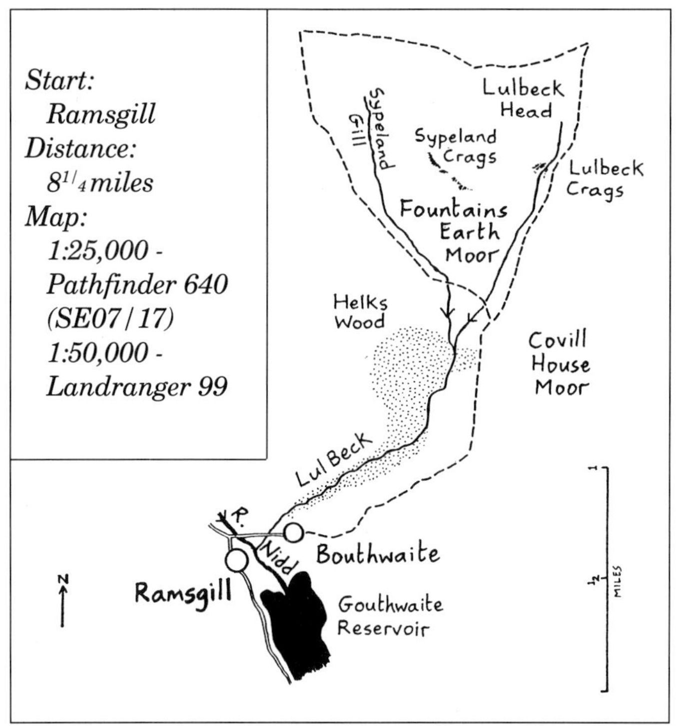

From Jenny Twigg to Sypeland Crags

The Yorke Arms occupies centre stage in Ramsgill

Heading for Fountains Earth Moor, with Sypeland Crags on the skyline

Boundary stone, Lulbeck Head

Gouthwaite Reservoir is very much a physical barrier in Nidderdale, for everything above it has a distinct dalehead feel: Ramsgill village sits at the head of Gouthwaite, beyond which the hills engulf all.

Even with a large ivy-clad hotel dominating the scene, Ramsgill remains a sleepy locale, surely little changed since shooting parties emerged from the Yorke's former lodge onto the spacious green, bound for umpteen brace on the moors above. A sultry late summer day saw me heading for those hazy heights, and as I left the village a colourful poster forewarned of a time-honoured rural event in preparation.

As every true West Riding rambler knows only too well, the Nidderdale moors are hardly awash with public paths, and so this rare opportunity to stride unhindered over the open spaces is one that should be firmly grasped. The narrow road to Bouthwaite supplies immediate interest in the form of another converted station house from the old Nidd Valley Light Railway.

While Ramsgill shared its station with its smaller neighbour, they shared less in monastic times as each was the site of a grange serving different houses. Though barely half a mile apart, Bouthwaite was in the hands of nearby Fountains Abbey, while Ramsgill's allegiance was to Byland, far across the Plain of York. A gable end by the church is all that remains of the monks' chapel.

Bouthwaite is very much the end of the road, and a solid track was my escalator to the moors. In the footsteps of members of both abbeys I gained height, and at the first junction a forlorn guidepost gave a clue to the fact that these green roads to Masham and Kirkby Malzeard were depicted on not-so-ancient maps as motorable: there is much to celebrate in the fact that they were never further improved. The level left arm soon ran along to a further junction, to which I would return after a triangular tour of Fountains Earth Moor.

Either option gives a bracing circuit, the firm going encouraging broad strides throughout the generous four miles ahead. The right branch runs free through the heather, with the gritstone range of

Sypeland Crags attracting attention. Proliferating in the rolling purple sea are old boundary and guidestones, much as on the greater expanses of the distant North York Moors. The base of the triangle runs past a shooting house from where the standing boulders of Jenny Twigg and her Daughter Tib can be glimpsed, while the third leg differs in not being a harder shooters' track but a magnificent green way largely enclosed by walls.

Sypeland Crags back on my skyline heralded a return to familiar ground, and having appraised both the crags and the big stones only from a restricted distance, I saw across the dale during my descent the side-valley of Ramsgill Beck, another of Nidderdale's forbidden corners. Glistening down-dale, meanwhile, were the still waters of Gouthwaite.

As I sauntered back across the green, the good ladies of the W.I. were setting out their cake stall and neatly arranging the home-grown greens: for my part, I was expected back for a trolley push round Sainsburys..... back to earth with a bump.

top:
Freedom of the Dales? - Jenny and Daughter from the shooting house

right:
In the flesh - Jenny Twigg and her Daughter Tib

40: SCAR HOUSE AND DALE EDGE

Start:
Middlesmoor
Distance:
9 miles
Map:
1:25,000 - Yorkshire Dales North / Central or Pathfinder 640 (SE07 / 17)
1:50,000 - Landranger 99

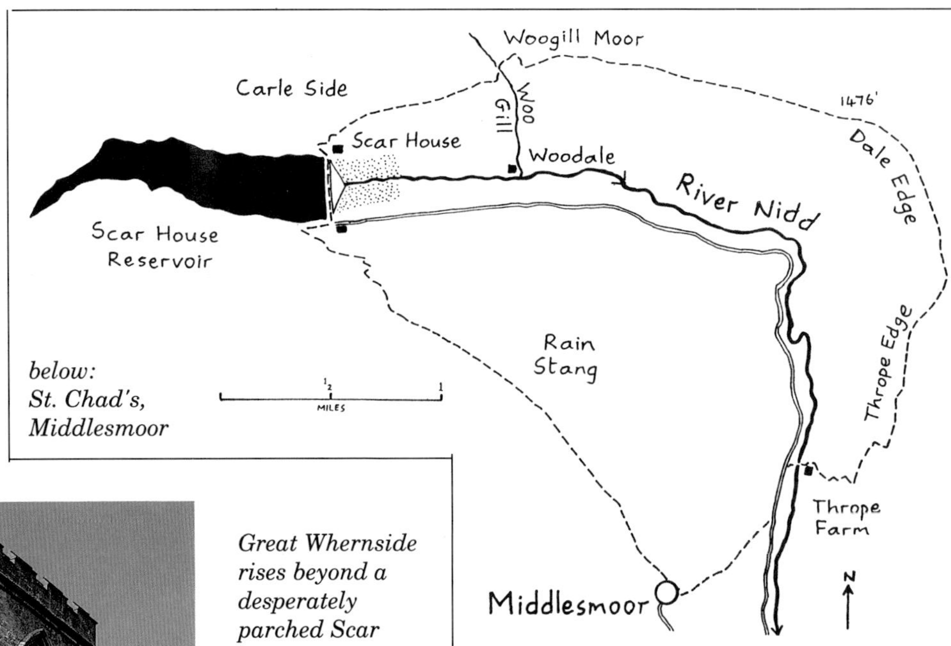

below: St. Chad's, Middlesmoor

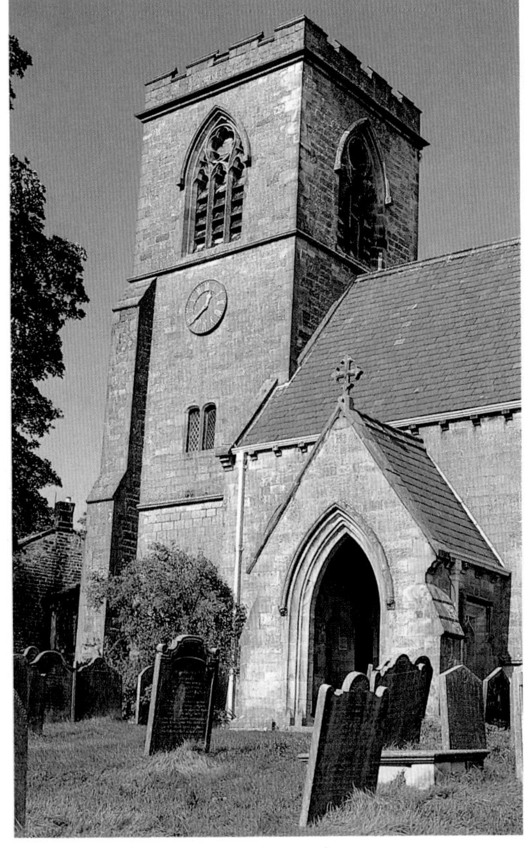

Great Whernside rises beyond a desperately parched Scar House Reservoir

High level walking, inviting tracks, wide-ranging views and an avoidance of complicated navigation combine to form a classic round, Exhibit A in Nidderdale's claim to National Park status.

Middlesmoor is in every sense Nidderdale's highest village. At little under a thousand feet, it sits brazenly on the great tongue of moorland keeping the upper dale away from its side valley of How Stean Beck. Little more than a hamlet, it nevertheless hides a wealth of secret ways and ginnels between its weathered cottages. From the platform of the

left:
Striding out along Dale Edge, Woogill Moor

below:
The great sweep of the upper dale seen from Dale Edge with the dark wall of Great Whernside overtopping the moorland of Rain Stang

churchyard it is master of all it surveys, and what is surveys is the green and pleasant land stretching down to Gouthwaite Reservoir and beyond. In marked contrast this walk chooses the opposite direction, and heads for the sterner stuff of the dalehead.

When the exhausted road reaches the last barn it wastes little time in calling it a day, and taking over is a wide track that inclines cautiously to the moorland of Rain Stang. No sooner does it escape the confinement of gritstone walls then it prepares for a steep drop, with the scene filled as in a big screen extravaganza by the seldom tramped slopes of Great and Little Whernside beyond the waters of Scar House Reservoir. The massive wall of the dam, built from stone quarried out of these very hillsides, gives a useful passage to the opposite slopes like some handily placed rope bridge over a deep gorge.

Downstream from Scar House the Nidd makes a bold sweep from east to south, and the enclosing arm of Dale Edge issues an invitation to stride through three ever-improving miles. Past sweeps of heather moor the luxuriant track reaches its zenith, as the green road to end them all glides round to a shooting house that resembles a place of worship. Its value as a landmark is greatly appreciated as it marks the start of a rapidly accomplished zigzag descent to Thrope Farm and the Nidd. Only a couple of minutes on the road - erstwhile trackbed of the old light railway - lead to a string of stiles mounting the fields to Middlesmoor, which will have changed as little in the last few hours as it has in as many decades.

Looking down-dale to Thrope Edge from the climb to Dale Edge

NOTES IN CONCLUSION

This book is founded on many years roaming the Dales, often to research walks for other books, but often simply pottering about with my family or enjoying more serious undertakings with like-minded friends.

The photographs were taken between 1983 and 1991, almost exclusively on Kodachrome 64 film but occasionally on Kodachrome 200. About half of those eventually chosen were taken during the course of 1990. Cameras used were Olympus OM10 and OM20 until both were replaced in 1989 by a Canon EOS 650. None of that 'I'm not an equipment freak, but I have half a dozen up-market cameras to choose from, use various professional films and a battery of light meters' nonsense here! Nor has a single effect filter ever been attached to my camera, as I am unimpressed by the likes of tobacco skies attempting to prop up a photograph that wasn't otherwise worth the taking. My greatest difficulty has always been a disinclination to hang around more than two minutes for suitable conditions, which time and again confirms my true guise as a walker first and a photographer second.

I would like to acknowledge the support of my wife Sandra, who, after breaking open the piggy bank for the Westmorland Way all those years ago, has entrusted far more in this ambitious venture into the 1990s; and also Aileen and Brian Evans at Carnmor for the benefit of their experience, and their invaluable advice and assistance with the book's production.

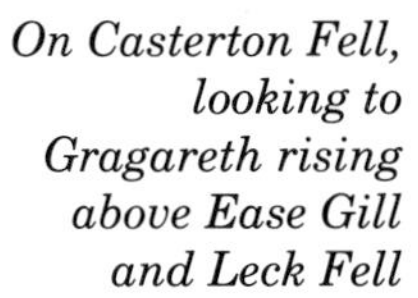

On Casterton Fell, looking to Gragareth rising above Ease Gill and Leck Fell

PAUL HANNON, born 1957, has been a writer of walkers' guidebooks since 1983, and four years later took great satisfaction in resigning from the Civil Service in order to concentrate on full-time walking and writing. His pocket-size books now cover much of the finest walking in Northern England, and the majority of them are based quite unashamedly on the hand-written format pioneered by the master, A. Wainwright.

Married with three children, he still lives in his home town of Keighley.

INDEX
Principal References : photographs in bold

Addlebrough ***126***, *128*, ***128-130***
Aire Head Springs *55*
Aire, River *46*, ***46***, ***47***, *55*
Airton ***46***, *46*, *48*
Angram *117*
Arant Haw *85*, ***85-88***
Arkengarthdale ***4***, *104*, ***105***
Arkle Beck ***106***, *106*
Arncliffe *30*, ***31***, ***32***
Arngill Force ***113***, *115*
Askrigg *125*
Aysgarth *122*, ***123***
  Falls *122*, ***122***, ***124***

Bainbridge *131*, ***133***
Bain, River *131*, ***133***
Barbon *75*, ***76***
Barden Moor *23*
Beamsley Beacon ***16***, ***43***
Beckermonds *38*, ***39***
Bell Busk *46*
Bewerley *144*
Black Force *90*, ***92***
Blakethwaite Smelt Mill ***110***, *111*
Blea Moor ***68***, *69*
Blease Fell ***90***
Bluecaster Side *80*, ***82***
Bolton Abbey *14*, *17*
Bolton Bridge *15*, ***16***
Bolton Castle *122*, ***123***
Bolton Hall *15*
Bolton Priory ***13***, ***15***, *15*
Booze ***4***, *104*
Borrow Beck ***79***, ***93***, *94*
Borrowdale ***79***, ***93***, *94*
Bouthwaite *152*
Brackenbottom *67*
Brants Gill Head *67*
Brimham Rocks *142*, ***142***, ***143***
Brownthwaite Pike ***76***, *76*
Buckden Pike ***28***
Bullpot Farm *76*
Bull Pot of the Witches *76*
Bunton Crushing Mill *111*

Calders ***85***, *85*
Calver Hill, ***2***, ***105***, ***106***
Cam High Road *132*
Carlin Gill ***89***, *89*
Carperby *122*
Casterton Fell *75*, ***77***, *157*
Castle Bolton ***121***, *122*
Cautley ***80***, *80*
  Crag ***80***, *80*
  Spout *80*, ***80***, ***83***, ***84***
CB Smelt Mill *106*
Combe Scar ***73***, *74*
Countersett ***132***, *132*
Cowside Beck ***58***
Cracoe *24*
  Fell ***23***, ***24***, *24*
Crag Hill ***77***
Crook *85*, ***86***
Crookrise Crag ***42-45***, *43*

Dale Edge ***155***, ***156***, *156*
Darnbrook *58*
  Fell *35*
Dee, River ***74***, *74*
Dent ***8***, ***72***, *72*
Dentdale *69-74*, ***71-73***
Dent Head *70*, ***70-71***

Eastby *44*
East Gill Force ***114***, *115*
Eden, River *139*
Embsay *15*, *42*
  Crag *43*, ***43***, ***45***
  Moor *44*

Feizor *63*, ***65***
Fell Beck *142*
Fell Head ***86***, ***87***, *92*
Flinter Gill ***72***, *74*
Force Gill ***69***
Fountains Earth Moor ***152***, *152*
Fountains Fell ***39***
Fremington Edge ***2***, ***103***, *104*, ***105***

Gordale Beck *53*, *55*, ***56***
Gordale Scar *53*, ***53-56***
Gouthwaite Reservoir ***141***, *149*, ***150***, *152*
Gragareth ***157***
Great Close *58*
  Scar *57*, ***59***
Great Dummacks ***84***
Great Pinseat *107*, ***109***
Great Whernside ***30***, ***154***, ***155***
Green Bell *96*, ***96***, ***98***, ***99***
Grimwith Reservoir *19*
Grinton *102*
  Lodge *102*, ***103***
  Moor ***2***, ***103***
  Smelt Mill *102*, ***102***, ***103***
Grisedale *139*
Guise Cliff ***145***, ***146***, *146*
Gunnerside *110*
  Gill ***110-112***, *111*

Halton Gill *37*
Hanlith *46*, ***48***, *55*
Hard Level Gill *107*
Hardraw *135*
  Force ***135***, *136*
Haw Crag *46*
Hawes *134*
Hawkswick *31*
  Moor *30*
Hell Gill *139*
  Force ***137***, *139*
Helwith Bridge *66*
Hesleden *34*
  Bergh ***33***, *34*
High Clint *134*, ***136***
High Crag Ridge ***144***
High Seat ***98***
High Way ***138***, *139*
Horse Head ***33***, *37*, ***39***
Horton in Ribblesdale *66*, ***67***

Ingleborough *37*, *66*, ***71***

Janet's Foss *53*
Jeffrey's Mount *94*, ***95***
Jenny Twigg and her Daughter Tib
 151, ***153***, *153*

Keld *115*, *116*, ***118***
Kettlewell ***26***, *26*, *30*, ***30***, ***32***
Kirkby Malham ***47***, *48*
Kisdon Force ***117***
Kisdon Hill *115*, *117*, ***117***

Langstrothdale *37*, ***38***, ***39***
Langthwaite *104*
Linghaw ***92***, *92*
Linton *23*, ***25***
Little Stainforth *63*
Litton *33*, ***34***
Littondale *30-38*
Low Borrow Bridge *93*
Lulbeck Head ***152***
Lune Gorge *94*, ***95***
Lune, River ***92***, ***94***, *94*, *97*
Lune's Bridge ***94***, *94*

Mabbin Crag ***79***, ***93***
Malham *49*, ***51***, *53*
 Cove *50*, ***50-52***
 Moor *57*
 Tarn *57*, ***57***, ***59***
 Water *55*, *57*
Mallerstang Edge ***98***, *139*
Mastiles Lane ***41***, ***54***, *55*
Middle Hill *20*, ***21***
Middle House *57*
Middlesmoor ***154***, *154*
Middleton Fell ***73***, *74*, ***77***
Mill Gill Force ***125***, *126*
Moorcock Inn *137*, ***138***
Moor End *26*
Muker *113*

Nappa Cross ***49***, *49*
Nappa Hall ***121***, *125*, ***126***
Newfield Bridge ***47***
Nidd, River ***148***, ***150***, *150*, *156*
North Gang Scar ***119***, *119*
Nursery Knot ***19***, *19*

Occupation Road *74*
Old Cote Moor *30*, ***30***, ***32***
Old Gang Smelt Mill ***107***, ***108***, *108*

Parceval Hall *20*
Pateley Bridge ***145***, *145*, *148*
Penyghent *34*, ***36***, *37*, ***39***, ***63***, ***66***, *66*
 Gill *34*, ***34***, ***36***
Pikedaw ***49***, *49*
Pike Hill ***134***, *135*, ***136***
Plover Hill ***39***
Posforth Gill ***18***, *18*
Pot Scar *63*, ***64***

Ramsgill ***151***, *151*
Raven's Gill ***147***
Ravenstonedale *96*, ***97***
Rawthey Bridge ***80***
Rawthey, River, *80*, ***83***
Reeth ***2***, ***104***, *104*
Ribblehead ***68***, *68*, *69*, ***71***
Ribble, River ***62***, *63*, ***65***, *66*, ***67***
Ribblesdale *62-67*
Rogan's Seat ***119***
Roundthwaite *94*
 Common *94*, ***95***

Scar House Reservoir ***154***, *156*
Scot Gate Ash Quarry ***149***, *149*
Sedbergh *85*
Sedbusk *135*
Semerwater *128*, ***128***, ***129***, ***131***, *131*,
 132
Settlebeck Gill *85*, ***86***
Settle-Carlisle Line ***68***, *69*, ***70***, ***71***,
 139, *139*
Sharp Haw ***44***
Simon's Seat *17-19*, ***17-19***, ***21***
Skirfare, River *30-32*, *34*, ***35***
Skyreholme 18-*20*, ***19***
The Slit ***31***, *31*
Smearsett Scar ***62***, *63*, ***64***
Smelthouses *142*
The Spout *90*, ***91***
Stackhouse *64*
Stainforth *62*
 Bridge ***62***, *63*, ***65***
 Force *63*, *64*, ***65***

Starbotton *28*, ***28***, ***29***
Strid Wood *15*, *18*
Stump Cross Caverns *19*
Surrender Bridge *107*
Surrender Smelt Mill *108*, ***109***
Swale Gorge *115*, *119*
Swale, River *115*, ***117***, *118*, ***119***
Swinner Gill *115*, ***116***, *119*
Sypeland Crags ***151***, ***152***, *152*

Thoresby Lane *123*
Thornton Rust ***129***, *130*
Thorpe *23*
 Fell ***22***, *24*
Thwaite *117*, ***118***
Trollers Gill *18*, *20*, ***21***
Turner Hill *139*

Uldale Head ***89***,
Ure, River ***122***, *123*, ***124***, *125*

Valley of Desolation *18*

Waterfall Gill *44*
Water Sinks *57*
Wath *149*, ***149***, ***150***
Watlowes *50*
Weets Top *55*
Wharfe, River ***14-16***, *15*, *18*, ***26***, ***28***,
 29, *30*, *38*, ***38***
Whernside ***68***, *69*
Whitfield Gill *125*, ***127***
Wild Boar Fell ***83***, ***138***, ***139***
Winder *85*, ***88***
Worton *128*

overleaf:
Winter afternoon above Malham